What Happens When You Let God

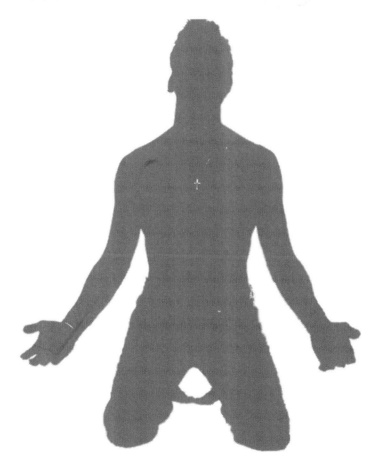

by Nick Arandes

Part I & II

©2008 SEDNARA Publishing

Order this book online at www.sednara.com
Most SEDNARA titles are also available at major online book retailers.
© Copyright 2008 Nick Arandes.

If you purchased this book without a cover you should be aware that this book may have been stolen property and reported as "unsold and destroyed" to the publisher. In such case neither the author nor the publisher has received any payment for this "stripped book."

This book contains copyrighted material. All rights reserved. No part of this book may be reproduced in any mechanical, photographic, or electronic process, or in the form of a phonographic recording nor may it be stored in a retrieval system, transmitted, or otherwise be copied for public or private use other than for a "fair use" as brief quotations embodied in articles and reviews-without prior written permission of the publisher and/or author. Violators of copyright law will be prosecuted.

Note for Librarians: A cataloguing record for this book is available from Library and Archives USA Printed in USA
ISBN-10:1477615946
ISBN-13:978-1477615942

We at SEDNARA believe that it is the responsibility of us all, as both individuals and corporations, to make choices that are environmentally and socially sound. You, in turn, are supporting this responsible conduct each time you purchase a SEDNARA book, or make use of our publishing services.

Our mission is to efficiently provide the world's finest, most comprehensive book publishing service, enabling every author to experience success. To find out how to publish your book, your way, and have it available worldwide, visit us online at www.CreateSpace.com

www.SEDNARA.com
638 Camino De Los Mares
Suite H130-135
San Clemente, CA 92673
email: info@fulfillyourdreams.com
ISBN-10:1477615946
ISBN-13:978-1477615942

> The intention of the author is only to offer information of a general nature to help you in your quest for personal growth. What is outlined in this book is practiced by the author on a daily basis. In the event you use any of the information contained in this book, the author and the publisher assume no responsibility for your actions. The author wants also to make clear that the principles outlined here, although based on the teachings of *A Course in Miracles*, does not make the author an authority on The Course. He is simply sharing his own understanding of what The Course teaches as well as his experiences as a result of practicing and applying the principles contained in The Course.

To order additional products or services visit:
www.TruthAndMiracles.com
www.WhatHappensWhenYouLetGod.com

Book cover designed, illustrations and formatting by the author.

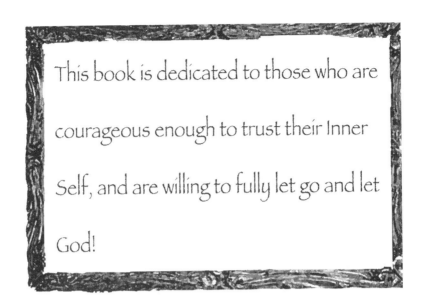

"Father, I give You all my thoughts today. I would have none of mine. In place of them, give me Your Own. I give You all my acts as well, that I may do Your Will instead of seeking goals which cannot be obtained, and wasting time in vain imaginings. Today I come to You. I will step back and merely follow You. Be You the Guide, and I the follower who questions not the wisdom of the Infinite, nor Love whose tenderness I cannot comprehend, but which is yet Your perfect gift to me."
-Lesson 233 A Course in Miracles

"I can of mine own self do nothing: as I hear, I judge: and my judgment is just; because I seek not mine own will, but the will of the Father which hath sent me."
[John 5:30]

When A Course in Miracles came into my life through a series of synchronistic events back in November of 2007, I was fortunate enough to have started it with two teachers who did not deviate from the non dualistic message of the course.

Even with the help of my teachers, it was almost impossible to not have the words filtered in some way by the ego's thought system. Therefore, the original version of the book, which consisted of three parts, has been actualized into the version that you now hold in your hands. I have left out the third part of the previous edition, which consisted of frequently asked questions.

Perhaps by the time you are reading this, the third part will have been formulated into a new book that reflects a more non dualistic understanding of the course as well.

In regards to this revised edition, the main message and practice is consistent with the previous edition. If you happen to have an older copy, I simply reworded some passages as well as took out anything that seemed dualistic in nature. My intention is to convey the non dualistic message of the course without tempting the mind of the reader with dualistic language.

This book still contains some dualistic aspects for practical application, comparison, and generalization purposes and is therefore in no way meant as a substitute nor an attempt to teach A Course in Miracles. The Course has only one Teacher; the One Who dictated it.

If the reader focuses on the main message of the book, even with the dualistic examples shared in the previous version, the experience of putting the principles into practice will be evident. So enjoy the content of this book and thank you for allowing me the opportunity to share my love in this form with you.

Praises

"What Happens When You Let God by Nick Arandes gives the reader <u>a guide to a practical use of the teachings of ACIM. I highly recommend this book</u> to everyone who wants to live life more happily and easily." **Gary Renard, Bestselling author of *The Disappearance of the Universe* and *Your Immortal Reality*.**

*"In his magnificent book, What Happens When You Let God, Nick asks What would happen if you let go and let God and then he becomes a Master guide helping us navigate our inner terrain with love as the safety net! <u>He embodies ACIM & offers guidance and clarity</u> to those of us who resonate with ACIM and journey with him. <u>He gives his attention to every detail of the Course, always consistent with the</u> **message** as revealed and never lets himself or us be sidetracked or distracted from the teaching by a mind that struggles with letting go and letting God! I love Nick's book <u>and I often carry it with me should I forget to remember who I really am</u>, and that, 'I am as God created me'!" Love,* **Carol Ann McVane**

Nick, just to let you know that I have 6 more pages to read of your book. <u>It has been excellent and a real down-to-earth approach to ACIM.</u> Talk about "when the student is ready". First, it was Nouk and Thomas' book, then Gary Renard's 2 books and then yours. Many thanks," **-Pat Hendy**

"Nick, I am reading your book What Happens When You Let God. <u>It is truly very inspiring and never fails to bring me a strong sense of peace.</u> Marianne Williamson and Wayne Dyer are two of my favorite authors, and I have to say that your book is in the same category with their books. Also, as far as its application to the Course in Miracles, <u>it really demonstrates all that which is possible through the simple act of forgiveness and the process of surrendering." **-Megan Green,** *Attorney*

"What Happens When You Let God by Nick Arandes <u>is a wonderful and simply practical guide to true forgiveness as taught in A Course In Miracles.</u> So whether you are a learned student of A

Course In Miracles or have never heard of it, this book will help guide you to a new life, free of suffering. I especially like the summary at the end of the book, which can be used as a daily reminder to live happily and easily." **-Linda Jean McNabb, Author of One Again: "A True Story of a Different Kind of Forgiveness"**

"Nick Arandes is a sincere and dedicated student of A Course in Miracles. <u>I gleaned some great insights in his book</u> What Happens When you Let God. Enjoy!" **-Sheryl Valentine, Author of "Oh My God, It's ME!"**

"What Happens When You Let God is a wonderfully down to earth sharing of the lived wisdom of A Course in Miracles. <u>Nick Arandes is a teacher and student of the Course who really walks his talk and it shows!</u> Full of love and encouragement, humor and insight, <u>we highly recommend this to anyone</u> who wants to experience what happens when you let God." **-Nouk Sanchez and Tomas Vieira, Authors of *"Take Me To Truth, Undoing the Ego"***

"NICK, Your Book, "What Happens When You Let God" is SUPER! Never have I seen **so** <u>much given in such a loving, caring way.</u> It is so comprehensive in providing core themes of A Course in Miracles...<u>it deserves to be a MUST reading for anyone who wants to go beyond the symbols,</u> concepts and words to the light and love of your own experiences so generously shared for all. THANK YOU FRIEND!" **-David Fishman, Host of *"ACIM Gather Radio"***

"Through What Happens When You Let God, author Nick Arandes gives us all the gift of marrying A Course in Miracles with practical application. Intimately sharing from his own stories of challenge, <u>Nick leads the reader through the dark tunnels of struggle to remember the hope which thrives within and beyond each obstacle to peace.</u> What Happens When You Let God is a comprehensive and prolific tool for applying A Course in Miracles to every stone the road of life may hurl. Thank you Nick for your willingness to share and lead the way." **-Pamela Silberman, Author of *"Simply Being: One Year with Spirit"***

More praises available upon request.

Content

Praises .... *ix*
Acknowledgements .... *xv*
A Word From The Author .... *xvii*
One Last Thing Before We Start .... *xix*
How The Story Began .... *xxiii*
Preface .... *xxv*
Introduction *1*
I Who You Really Are *9*
II The Gift From God *25*
III God Did Not Create The World That We See *31*
IV The Birth of False Idols *39*
    The Ego's Plan for Its Survival 41
    Our Deep Yearning For Helping Others 42
Most Predominant Beliefs, i.e. Illusions *45*
    Visualization 45
    Goal Setting 50
    Developing a Plan of Action 51
    God Helps Those Who Help Themselves 52
    Things Happen In Divine Timing 53
    You Must Know What You Want.. 54
    What Is In It For Me... 55
    Perception Makes Projection 56
    Nothing Has A Meaning Unless You Give It A Meaning 58
    People Know What To Do But Don't Do What They Know 59
    Motivation 61
    The Why Is More Important Than The How 61

Do What Others Have Done And Experience The Same Results 62

To be, do, have, or to do, have, be, what was the question? 64

Your Beliefs Determine Your Destiny 66

If You Do What's Hard, Life Becomes Easy 69

Human Beings Do What They Do Because Of The Need To Avoid Pain And The Desire To Seek Pleasure 71
    The illusion of needing significance 72
    The illusion of needing certainty 73
    The illusion of needing uncertainty 74
    The illusion of needing love/connection 74
    The illusion of needing to grow 74
    The illusion of needing to contribute 75

V This Thing Called Suffering 81

VI The Power of Forgiveness 87

VII The Process 93

VIII Letting Go of Control Thru The Development of Trust 105

  Stage 1: The Period of Undoing 106

  Stage 2: The Period of Sorting Out 107

  Stage 3: The Period of Relinquishment 108

  Stage 4: The Period of Settling Down 109

  Stage 5: The Period of Unsettling 110

  Stage 6: The Period of Achievement 112

IX The Present Moment 115

X The Story Has Been Told 119

Introduction Part II 129

XI Health & Healing 133

XII Wealth & Abundance 139

XIII Career 149

XIV Feelings & Emotions 155

XV Helping Others & The World 161

XVI Relationships	167
XVII True Forgiveness	171
Conclusion Parts I & II	177
About the Author	191
Additional Support	193
Suggested Readings	195
Additional Resources	197
Book Nick To Speak	199
Testimonials	201

A Course in Miracles' second edition consist of the *Preface*, part I, also known as the *Text*, part II, the *Workbook for Students,* part III, the *Manual for Teachers*, and finally the *Clarification of Terms*. The third edition of the *Course* has two additional addendums, which consist of *The Song of Prayer* and *Psychotherapy: Purpose, Process and Practice*. That's the only difference between versions two and three. There is an earlier version, which is referred to as the *Original Edition*. The abbreviations below apply to the second and third version because approximately five chapters were omitted from the original version. However, the teachings contained in each version of *A Course in Miracles* remained *consistent* and *unaltered*.

Abbreviations used for easier reference to specific passages:

T: Text (Part I of the Course)
W: Workbook for Students (Part II of the Course)
M: Manual for Teachers (Part III of the Course)
C: Clarification of Terms
S: Song of Prayer (An addendum to A Course in Miracles)
in: Introduction
pI: Part I
pII: Part II

Example:

T-29.V.5:4-8 means:
Text, Chapter 29, Section V, Paragraph 5 Sentences 4 to 8.
W-pI.100.2:3 means:
Workbook for Students, Part I, Lesson 100, Paragraph 2, Sentence 3.

M-4.2:3 means:
Manual for Teachers, Chapter 4, Paragraph 2, Sentence 3.
T-25.In.3:1-2 means:
Text, Chapter 25, *Introduction*, Paragraph 3, Sentences 1 and 2.
C-in.4:1-5 means:
Clarification of Terms, Introduction, Paragraph 4, Sentences 1 to 5.

Acknowledgements

First, and foremost, I want to thank the *Creator,* not only for giving me the inspiration to write the words contained in this book, but also for the *courage* to share these principles that have brought peace into my life. I want to thank the following people for sharing their unconditional love, their skills and support in helping me make this book possible. They are Dianne Jones, Mayme Smith and Carol Ann MacVane for their exceptional work in proofreading this book while honoring and respecting my writing style. Pamela Silberman for being so kind in helping me write the *A Word From The Author* page of this book.

I want to thank one of the greatest gifts in my life, *Dawn Jackson* for being my teacher, my loving friend, for supporting me every step of the way. Had it not been for her I don't think I would have become the kind of individual who could write this book. I may be a good teacher and writer, but she is a true *example.* "*I thank you Dawn for being such a big part of my life. I know words can't describe the deep love and appreciation I feel for you.*"

Along this road I have encountered many setbacks, yet, God always had an angel ready to help carry me through times when I did not know where my next meal would come from or where I would rest my head at night, or to just listen to me without judging me. In no specific order some of these names are, John Ortiz, Debbie Dobbins, Sharron Babb, Aaron Kleinerman, Susan and Ryder Collins, which by the way, in my humble opinion I have to say that Ryder Collins must be an advanced soul disguised as a twenty year old kid, for every time I talked with him I was baffled by the wisdom that came out of his mouth. Probably without him knowing this, he has been a great teacher to me. Continuing on I thank Ron D. Blair, Gerald Collins, Armand and Angelina, Jodi LaChance, Lori Woodley, Mike Garcia, Dr. Sheryl Valentine, Staci Schubert, and someone who had it not been for our encounter almost twenty years prior to me writing this book, my spiritual journey would not have begun, and that person is Mary DiPadova. I also want to acknowledge every single person who attended *A Course in Miracles'* study group every Sunday at the *Agape International Spiritual Center* for being such great teachers to me.

I want to honor the two people who raised me – my late mother, Iris Arandes and my late grandmother, Juanita Arandes, for all the great lessons of life that they provided to me. I am so grateful that they never put up barriers to my creativity, always allowing me to explore, even when my grades in school weren't the best. I thank everyone else who has touched my life that I would love to mention here but if I did I would have to write another book.

And of course, *I LOVE YOU* and from the depth of my being I truly *THANK YOU*, for allowing me the opportunity to share the words contained in this book with you.

With sincere love and appreciation,

Nick Arandes
A.K.A. The *Radical* Kid!

A Word From The Author

Dear Reader,

      Before proceeding, I would like to issue a slight disclaimer. As a native of Puerto Rico, although I have a pretty good command of the English language, there is a noticeable conversational style within my writing. This is important to note, because while in the process of this book's publication, some editors made suggestions that this style should change. However, as the author, I decided to keep all writings as first recorded because I feel this style is the best representative of me.

      To those who are not familiar with my work, I believe that life's progress is most beneficial when we choose to follow our inner guidance. Paraphrasing German philosopher Friedrich Nietzsche, he said it best: *"There is your way, and my way, for the way - does not exist!"* Likewise, one of the greatest compliments I received about this book stated: *"Hi Nick. Got the book. I am reading it. Like talking to a friend. Thanks for writing it."* -Louise F.

      Therefore, it is not my intention to sound like a highly intellectual author. More importantly, I wish to simply share from my heart. I would also like to bring to your attention that this book is based on my experiences as I practice the principles taught through *A Course in Miracles*. You'll notice that quotes from the Course are prefaced by me saying, "*A Course in Miracles* reminds me" as opposed to "*A Course in Miracles* states." I choose to use this format because I honor the many paths available and recognize that *A Course in Miracles* may not be the only answer for humankind.

      Some people may feel drawn to read the Bible while others may resonate best with the Qur'an or the Bhagavad Gita, the Torah or the Kabbalah. We each receive the message most necessary through walking our own path. To me, the Course is merely a tool upon the path rather than the path itself. Regardless of the tools used on our chosen path, I believe we must practice what we learn as opposed to only collecting a theoretical understanding of any teaching. Therefore, my statements of concepts from *A Course in Miracles* will only have limited impact without actual practice.

Personally, I hope to relate to you how my walking the walk brought a greater gift than merely talking the talk. Now, let us embark on this journey together, it will be a journey of Spirit. As you read the following pages, imagine yourself sitting on a sandy beach in my native island of Puerto Rico. Envision yourself looking at the ocean as this new friend, me, sits next to you and begins to have a conversation that sounds like this...

One Last Thing Before We Start

Recently I received a wonderful article by Hugh Prather written back in 1999: Although was very extensive, one of the paragraphs that caught my attention was:

"Does this mean those who lecture or write about the Course have turned down a dark side road? Certainly not. Does it mean that anyone who loves discussing metaphysical ideas has lost his or her way? Certainly not. But it does mean that those who coat themselves in spiritual concepts run the risk of thinking that they are the concepts. It's not hard to notice that the people in our culture who are conspicuously devout and talk continuously about God usually begin to take on an all-knowing, all-seeing attitude. In other words, in their own minds they have become the God they profess."

That's why I keep asking myself, why is it that I find myself writing books, and speaking, even when I am still facing my own darkness? Shouldn't I have it altogether before I can teach? And the answer I keep getting is that I am doing it to remind myself of what "I" need to learn.

It is like someone who was born with the innate desire to surf, and is destined to be a great surfer, but in his mind he does not want to get on the surfboard until he think he can master it first. Well, that will never happen. He has to get on that surfboard, fall out of it many times, before he can master it. And yes, at the beginning, he may hit people with the surfboard for not having mastered the right balance and control. He also have to ride all kinds of waves until he gets a better feel for them, and eventually, he will reach his destination, which is to become the great surfer he is meant to be.

This came to mind because since I have written books, and for some reason speaking is something I enjoy doing, and based on the feedback I have received, I guess I must be getting better at it, what I often remind people of, is that I experience the same challenges everybody else does. I do not claim that I talk to Jesus, or that I have achieved some kind of enlightenment, or that I am a guru, or pride myself on having reached some kind of spiritual level of consciousness, or that I know something, because in reality I don't. I am moving towards achieving a state of unconditional love, but I guess that when that happens, people will naturally sense it, and at that point my writings and speaking are just stuff that I do.

I don't know if tomorrow I may feel guided to take my facebook profile down, get rid of my websites, move to a little town, get a job and live a happy life there. I don't know what the future holds for me. I just keep writing, and sharing, and trusting that hopefully, what I am doing is what I am supposed to be doing. And like the surfer, before I get to that place of complete unconditional love, for me, writing about it, and talking about it is one way of getting on that surfboard for the first few thousand times. And along the way, some people may experience my ego and may think, "who the hell is this guy teaching A Course in Miracles?"

But as I keep practicing, and my love keeps flourishing, some people may say, "this guy really walk his talk." But to get to that place, it requires, first and foremost, willingness to choose again; to choose love over and over and over and over again and again and again, until I have experienced all sorts of waves, just like the surfer. Because even if he can master a particular kind of wave, it does not mean he is able to ride every single wave. But the more he is exposed to different kinds of waves, the better he is equipped to maintain a good sense of balance in all circumstances.

I am very grateful for the journey I am on. But I do have to say, I have had to face a lot of darkness, and still do in many different areas. I am becoming better equipped to handle what comes my way, but I am still practicing, and as long as I am in what appears to be a body, the practice will never stop. My sense of balance may be more steady, but that does not mean I will not be faced with experiences that may rock my boat.

So if you like my writings and my speaking, I thank you, and I hope that in some way I am able to serve you through the use of these particular talents and gifts I seem to have. But do not make the mistake of putting me on a pedestal, because if you do, you are now turning me into what A Course in Miracles refers to as a "false idol."

Trust me when is say that YOU are the guru you have been searching for. And my writings are simply pointing you in the direction to where you must always look; within your Self!

I love you!

How The Story Began

In 1995 I wrote the following; *"My purpose in life is to bring joy, happiness and encouragement to every person whom I come into contact with; to devote my entire life to the development and growth of my spiritual, mental and physical capacities, so that I can serve as an example to others. To help everyone see the greatness that resides within them that will allow them to live their dreams so that they can share the fruit of their endeavors with their loved ones as well as humanity."*

Little did I know that the line, *"so that I can serve as an example to others"* would turn out to be completely different from what I had expected. Thirteen years later, after being homeless and broke numerous times, having filed for bankruptcy, being diagnosed with a thyroid tumor, and no longer having a fulfilling career, on Sunday, February 17 of 2008, I was asked to leave the place where I was staying.

With maybe twenty dollars to my name, and enough gas to go to church, I met with my *Course In Miracles'* study group in the afternoon. As a result of me *practicing* the teachings of The Course, in the midst of my challenging experience, I was feeling very joyful, happy and peaceful. From that space, this is what I said after hearing one other student's personal concern. *"Right now I am broke, don't know what I am going to eat, don't even know where I am going to rest my head tonight. However, I can guarantee that there is a millionaire somewhere in this world, who has everything he has ever wanted, yet he is probably drowning himself in either alcohol, drugs, sex, may be dealing with depression, or even just one step away from committing suicide, who would give everything he has, in exchange for the peace that I have."*

At the end of the meeting, without me asking for anything, one of the students handed me some money, and another one told me that she had an extra room in her house that I could use for a few days while I was getting myself back on my feet.

So the story began...

Preface

> **"Think not the limits you impose on what you see can limit God in any way."**
> -*A Course in Miracles [Text: chapter 26, section II, paragraph 3, sentence 5]*

> **"But Jesus beheld them, and said unto them, With men this is impossible; but with God all things are possible."**
> -*Bible [Matthew: chapter 19, verse 26]*

I would like to share something I wrote at a time when I felt fearful, confused and alone. I simply picked up my notebook and the following words came through.

> God: *"Be still and know that I am God. When you read these words, how do you feel?"*
> Nick: "Peaceful, calm."
> God: *"From this place, simply sit down and listen. Just be quiet and know that I am handling everything for you, Nick. I am the One taking care of all of your needs, making sure that every happy thought that arises through, manifests. I am peace, I am calmness, I am still, I am joy, I am love, I am clarity, I am life! Read these words often, Nick. Know that in this moment and through eternity, Nick and I are One. Be still and know that I am God. Be still and know that I am God. Be still and know that I am God."*

Whether I was talking to God or myself is irrelevant. I simply trusted what I wrote. My intention is that by the time you finish reading this book, you will not only understand what you just read, but if you choose, it will be a way of life for you, just as it is for me.

So the question is; ***What happens when you let God?*** First and foremost you experience peace. From that space you become open and receptive to the still voice within that wants only for you to be happy. You feel that you are fully supported and completely provided for. You get to experience love, peace, happiness, joy, wisdom, and abundance as your *natural* state of being. You experience fulfillment, you live your life purposefully. *A Course in Miracles* asks the question: *"Can you imagine what it means to have no cares, no worries, no anxieties, but merely to be perfectly calm and quiet all the time?* **T-15.I.1:1** However, be aware that before that takes place, your world will probably be turned upside down for reasons that will be explained in detail throughout the book. To give you an idea, speaking from experience, when I truly made the decision to let go and let God, my whole world started to literally fall apart. In hindsight however, I now realize what was happening.

> *...in order to align yourself with the thought system of God or Spirit, you must first trust; surrender; have faith. The thought system of the world, on the other hand, is rooted in control.*

When we let go and let God, two complete opposite thought systems start to collide. I did not say two different thought systems, I said two *completely opposite* thought systems. These two thought systems I am referring to are the thought system of God or Spirit and the thought system of the world. *A Course in Miracles* reminds me: *"The way out of conflict between two opposing thought systems is clearly to choose one and relinquish the other."* **T-6.V.B.5:1** So the difference between the two, is that in order to align yourself with the thought system of God or Spirit, you must *first* trust; surrender; have faith. The thought system of the world, on the other hand, is rooted in *control*.

So letting go and letting God is synonymous with letting go of control. Now you may ask; *"But if I let go and let God by releasing control, why would my life have to fall apart?"* Your life *does not* have to fall apart. In fact, it will simply start falling *together* for the very first time, even when it doesn't appear to be that way. And that is because in order for you to experience your True Self, the part of you that is infinite abundant, pure love, perfect, whole and complete, you first have to let go of whatever beliefs, notions, and ideas you have made up about yourself, and be *willing* to let go of *everything* you consider to be of importance to you. The reason being is that *nothing* in this world is important; as you will soon discover after reading the chapters that follow.

Does this mean you have to live in a cave and become a monk? Unless that is your life's calling, no. Does it mean you cannot have fun in life, nor have nice things, etc.? Not at all, as a matter of fact, the paradox is, that when we let go of whatever we try to hang on to, we then open the doors for more to show up in our lives. Not that this is what this book is about, yet, unless people are willing to let go of that which they are so attached to, aside from the fact that they will not enjoy it because of fear of loosing it, they won't be able to have the *direct experience* of realizing that *everything* they struggle so hard to acquire, *they already have.*

So in letting go and letting God, not only are you given the opportunity to examine your beliefs and concepts of truth, but also to *transcend* them. You literally become open to the guidance that is available to you in each and every moment. Bottom line is, you have spent your whole life doing it your way, now is the time to try God's way. The good news is that you need to do *nothing* but to *let go and let God!*

Be the change you want to see in the world because...

Part I
Foundation

Introduction

"Salvation is no more than a reminder this world is not your home. Its laws are not imposed on you, its values are not yours. And nothing that you think you see in it is really there at all."
-A Course in Miracles [Text: chapter 25, section VI, paragraph 6, sentence 1]

"My kingdom is not of this world: if my kingdom were of this world, then would my servants fight..."
-Bible [John: chapter 18, verse 36]

Before we begin our journey together, I would like to share a bit about my background. Although I have been on a spiritual path my whole life, without even being aware of it, around 1986 is when my process began. For me, it was not a choice I made based on inspiration or insight, but out of *desperation* and *pain*. I was involved in a very painful romantic relationship. And no matter what she said or did, it seemed impossible for me to be happy. Every prior relationship

I had would bring up a lot of guilt and pain. And there was nothing I could do in order to rid myself of those painful feelings.

In the midst of our despair, she happened to pick up the newspaper and saw an ad about some kind of a mind control method. I did not know anything about the organization that was offering it. All I knew was that the words *mind control* captured my attention. My level of desperation was so strong that I did not care about how much it would cost. At that point, anything I thought could get rid of the demons that were plaguing my mind would do, for I had tried therapy in the past and it was not working for me.

After attending that course, I was introduced later to what they refer to as achieving an alpha state of mind. I learned that was another form of meditation. It was a two-week class and my mind was so agitated that for me, trying to quiet it only brought more and more frustration. However, something deep within would not let me not to continue practicing. It got to a point where I would meditate sometimes five times a day or more.

Seminar after seminar I attended. I studied with some of the most influential people in the areas of religion, spirituality, metaphysics, quantum physics, business, relationships and everything in between. I've seen the movies, practiced the exercises, mantras, crystals, affirmations, visualizations, I've done treasure mapping, I've gone to healers, tarot readers, mediums, psychics – I could go on forever. I even ended up working for over a year for a well-known author and trainer. Many teachers, gurus and self-help leaders have similar backgrounds; however, I differ from most because I am not using mine as a way to impress you with my resume but as a way to let you know that I spent my whole life looking up to *false idols*.

Many of them are very well-meaning I might add, yet all they taught me was to keep looking for answers where they can never be found. Meanwhile, I kept hearing, *"The answers are within,"* over and over again. Yet, those who continued to promote that truth, always had some kind of an answer; some kind of a tool to help me find answers. Pretty much, every course I took had some sort of hidden agenda, whether it was through meditation, mantras, hard work, determination, visualization, focus, weekly meetings, it was all about teaching me how to get or manifest what I want. *None of it* was about letting go and trusting. It was all about some sort of *control*. This seemed to be the central message I received from every teacher, healer, and guru. It was also the same message I received from every course, seminar and workshop I attended. When I felt my life was not working, I was taught that *"I"* needed to do something in order to change it or fix it. But what if the reason my life was not working was because *"I"* was trying to *do* something in order to change it or fix it? And what if the change I was trying to make happen could end up being more disastrous than beneficial?

A Course in Miracles reminds me: *"Some of your greatest advances you have judged as failures, and some of your deepest retreats you have evaluated as success."* **T-18.V.1:6** Think about it. How many times have you ended up getting what you prayed for, realizing later that what you thought would bring you happiness or fulfillment ended up being one of your biggest curses? Yet, looking back at your life, how many times have the seeming failures turned out to be your greatest blessings?

> *When I felt my life was not working, I was taught that "I" needed to do something in order to change it or fix it. But what if the reason my life was not working was because "I" was trying to do something in order to change it or fix it?*

Following one disappointment after another, I finally gave up. *That's when I was ready.* At the beginning I said that in 1986 was when my spiritual journey began. After being sick and tired of the way my life was going, even after twenty years of studying with every spiritual teacher, coach, minister, shaman, healer, guru, expert, seminar leader and trainer that crossed my path, on November 2007 I did something I never imagined I would ever do. I took every single book, tape, DVD, CD, *everything* I owned in the area of human, business and spiritual development, and I am talking from spirituality, religion, metaphysics to business, positive thinking, goal-setting, success and everything else in between, put everything I owned in two big boxes and gave it all to the Salvation Army. I literally gave away thousands and thousands and thousands of dollars worth of information.

On that day is when my *real* commitment to my spiritual growth happened. That is when I started to *truly* let go and let God. From that space, I was led to the teachings of *A Course in Miracles*. What attracted me to The Course is that it is *not* a religion, nor a how to book, not even a road map to help me find or even look for answers. All it did was lead me to the understanding that *no possible intellectual answer* can guide me to freedom. And there is a reason for that, which this book will address later on. For now I would like to share the introduction of *A Course in Miracles* just so that you get an idea of what The Course is about. Before doing so, I invite you to keep the following in mind. The principles contained herein can be applied and utilized by anyone *without* having to be a student of The Course. All that is required is a genuine open heart and *willingness* to let the love that is within you to express itself. Simple? Yes. Easy? We'll see.

The introduction to *A Course in Miracles* reads:

This is A Course in Miracles. It is a required course. Only the time you take it is voluntary. Free will does not mean that you can establish the curriculum. It means only that you can elect what you want to take at a given time. The Course does not aim at teaching the meaning of love, for that is beyond what can be taught. It does aim, however, at removing the blocks to the awareness of love's presence, which is your natural inheritance. The opposite of love is fear, but what is all-encompassing can have no opposite.

This course can therefore be summarized up very simply in this way;

Nothing real can be threatened.
Nothing unreal exists.

Herein lies the peace of God.

I would like to share with you my understanding of that introduction, especially after reading The Course and putting the principles into practice.

This is A Course in Miracles. It is a required course. Only the time you take it is voluntary.

Depending on where you are in your life, the time comes, hopefully sooner than later, when you realize that nothing this world has to offer will ever satisfy you. That's when most people either experience major breakdowns, find themselves dealing with mild or severe depression, some try to hide their feelings behind addictions such as alcoholism, overeating, sex, drugs, overworking, watching excessive television, they try all sorts of therapy, some may even end up committing suicide.

That's what is meant by it is a *required* course. Because when we finally get down on our knees, in order to pull ourselves out of our darkness, we need a power *greater* than ourselves to help us through. Getting down on our knees is another way of saying that we are *ready to let go and let God*. From this point, some may decide to take The Course or choose whatever path *out of many* that will help point them in the direction of uncovering who they really are. That's what is meant by, *only the time you take it is voluntary*. It is voluntary because nobody is forcing us to take The Course. The question is, how long do we want to continue suffering before we make the decision to let go and let God?

Free will does not mean that you can establish the curriculum. It means only that you can elect what you want to take at a given time.

The only free will you have is the will to choose God by employing the principles taught either in The Course or whatever spiritual practice that would lead you to real awakening, or choose your problems. Just for the sake of congruency, since we are talking about The Course, let's say you have decided to choose The Course, you can decide what part of The Course you are ready to commit to. Because The Course is clear that the *only* thing that will bring you *permanent* happiness, peace, joy and fulfillment is if you remember Who you really are. Since the awakening process has to be gradual, the lessons you are ready for will resonate with you at your present level of awareness, others may take time. That's why it says; *"you can elect what you want to take at a given time."*

The Course does not aim at teaching the meaning of love, for that is beyond what can be taught. It does aim, however, at <u>removing the blocks to the awareness of love's presence, which is your natural inheritance.</u>

The Course here is making a very powerful point. Since the meaning of love cannot possibly be taught because that goes *beyond* intellectual understanding, all The Course is doing is <u>assisting you</u> in <u>removing</u> the <u>blocks</u> that are not allowing you to have the <u>direct experience</u> of the love's presence that is within. In other words, *who you really are*, is *already* perfect love, therefore you *cannot* be taught that which you already are. However, <u>you can recognize it</u> by <u>removing all the blocks (fears) that you have made up</u> which are not allowing you to experience your *True* nature.

The opposite of love is fear, but what is all-encompassing can have no opposite.

This course can therefore be summarized up very simply in this way;

Nothing real can be threatened.
Nothing unreal exists.

Herein lies the peace of God.

In the next chapter, I will share my understanding of what the last few lines of The Course's introduction mean, because at this point you'll need a bit more of a foundation before you can grasp what they are trying to say.

So even though this book, and my life now, is grounded in the teachings of *A Course in Miracles*, I want to make something *very clear*. I am *not* implying nor suggesting that The Course is the way or the only path to spiritual awakening. It just happened to be a path, *out of many* I should say, that I resonated with the most; one that has finally led me to specific answers I have been searching for all my life- --*without* actually giving me the answers. And that is because The Course leads us to the answers that cannot be taught nor explained, they can only be *experienced*. That's why The Course says: *"The curriculum The Course proposes is carefully conceived and is* *explained, step by step, at both the theoretical and practical levels. It emphasizes application rather than theory. It specifically states that 'a universal theology is impossible, but a universal **experience** is not only possible but **necessary**.'"* **ACIM Preface**

This book will *not* attempt to offer any kind of answers, for that would be in direct conflict with the way God communicates with you. Simply read the book and watch the answers *reveal* themselves through you. My intention is to share from experience and to help remind you that you'll *never* find answers out in the world. *A Course in Miracles* reminds me: *"Within the world the answers merely* **raise another question***, though they leave the first unanswered."* **T-27.IV.7:4**

I am also using this book to remind you that wherever you are is exactly where you need to be, that everything is okay. *A Course in Miracles* reminds me: *"All things work together for good. There are no exceptions..."* **T-4.V.1:1-2** Also from the scriptures: *"And we know that all things work together for good to them that love God, to them who are the called according to his purpose."* **[Roman 8:28]** So even if you are dealing with a health issue or emotional, financial, social challenge, whatever the case may be, your life is unfolding *perfectly* as it should. And when you finish reading this book what I just said will not only make perfect sense, it will help you appreciate the *gift* within your current experience.

I will once again remind you, that as you embark on this journey of self-discovery, the world as you know it will shift, and the experience(s) you'll have can be overwhelming at times and for many people, very fearful. Yet, they are but part of a beautiful process, one where you are about to discover an aspect of your being so *magnificent*, so *amazing*, so *powerful*, so *glorious*, so *precious*, so *loving*, so *beautiful* that words *cannot* describe it. Yet, in order to have that experience, you need to be *open*. You have to be *willing* to let go of all that you *think* you know.

An old story is told about a professor who was extremely knowledgeable about eastern philosophy and was very interested in studying with a particular teacher. After having the opportunity to meet with the teacher, the professor was so excited that he wanted to impress him with all that he knew. The teacher softly asked, *"Would you like a cup of tea?"* The professor nodded yes while he continued talking. After the teacher started pouring tea in the cup, eventually the tea began to overflow, pouring onto the professor's pants. At that point the professor said, *"Excuse me but the cup is already full."* The teacher smiled slightly and said, *"Exactly, just like the cup, your mind is so full of what it knows, that there is no room for something new to get in."*

A Course in Miracles reminds me: "Those who remember always that they know nothing, and who have become willing to learn everything, will learn it. But **whenever they trust themselves**, they will not learn. **They have destroyed** their motivation for learning by **thinking** they already know." **T-14.XI.12.:1-3** When you realize that you know nothing, only then will you have access to knowledge. The knowledge that leads you to freedom: the freedom that can only be experienced when you remember **Who you really are.**

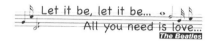

I
Who You Really Are

"The statement 'God created man in his own image and likeness' needs reinterpretation. 'Image' can be understood as 'thought,' and 'likeness' as 'of a like quality.' God did create spirit in His Own Thought and of a quality of His Own. There is nothing else."
-A Course in Miracles [Text: chapter 3, section V, paragraph 7, sentence 1]

"And God said, Let us make man in our image, after our likeness: and let them have dominion over the fish of the sea, and over the fowl of the air, and over the cattle, and over all the earth, and over every creeping thing that creepeth upon the earth."
-Bible [Genesis 1, verse 26]

Who are you? Have you ever asked yourself this question? When I did, first I thought I was my name. I am Nick. As a kid, I thought I was the son of my mother Iris and the grandson of my grandmother Juanita. I thought I was a friend to others. As I went to school, I thought I was a student. When I took flying lessons, I thought I was a licensed private pilot. As I started to do comedy, I thought I was a comedian. As I started to play music, I thought I was a musician. As I started to speak and write books, I thought I was a speaker and an author. Not only that, when I was happy, I thought I was happy. When I was sad, I thought I was sad. When I was having financial challenges, I thought I was broke. When I had money, I thought I was prosperous. Do you see a pattern here? I was equating my sense of self with what I was doing, feeling or having, not realizing these were just labels I placed on myself in order for me to have a sense of *identity*.

The thing is, no matter what label you choose to come up with, "I am rich, poor, happy, sad, a friend, a musician, a lawyer, a carpenter, a doctor, someone who is depressed, a wife, a husband, pretty, ugly, confident, inadequate" and I can go on forever, all of these are not really who you are. These are nothing but some of the *blocks* you have made up in order to cover up your *True* Self. A Course in Miracles reminds me: "*The 'Little I' seeks to enhance itself by external approval, external possessions and external 'love.'* **The Self That God created needs nothing.** *It is forever complete, safe, loved and loving. It seeks to share rather than to get; to extend rather than protect.*" **ACIM Preface**

So what is your True Self? In simple terms, it is *extraordinarily beyond description*. Words cannot describe it, because it is *beyond* intellectual understanding. In order for you to even get a sense of your True Self, one thing must be understood. And that is, who you are is *not* your body, not even your emotions or experiences. Who you are is *not* physical. It is *beyond* physical; it is *invisible, untouchable*, it is *pure love*. It is *Oneness*. It is *Real*. And what is meant by *Real* has nothing to do with what your eyes can see or your senses perceive. That is why *A Course in Miracles* reminds me: "*The body cannot know. And while you limit your awareness to its tiny senses, you will not see the grandeur that*

> *So what is your True Self? In simple terms, it is extraordinarily beyond description. Words cannot describe it, because it is beyond intellectual understanding.*

surrounds you." **T-18.VIII.2:1-2** So, does that mean we are energy, or Spirit?

Some may say that our essence is energy, while others say that it is spirit, and still others say we are both. We could say that we are Spirit if we stop trying to give it human attributes. For example, when some people say they see angels or spirits, for most they see them as bodies. Bodies that may be floating or bodies with wings, or a face, half bodies, whatever the case may be, they see figures that look like human beings. I am certainly not denying what they are seeing, because for all I know, Spirit can appear in many forms, especially one that we can understand. But to define who we are by such images can't be accurate, because if you see two images, you are not seeing oneness; you are seeing separation, which is no different than what the world of the physical looks like. That's why I keep saying that who you are is *beyond* intellectual understanding. Since this book is not about figuring out what Spirit is, an attempt to try to explain or understand it can keep you going around in circles *forever*. So let's just move on to the next word, energy.

When my spiritual journey began in the mid-eighties I was introduced to the concept of everything being energy. That allowed me to open up to this notion that maybe what we see may not necessarily be real or true. However, I still had doubts because a great part of me had a lot invested in the belief that the world I see with my physical eyes is real. Therefore, from a spiritual/metaphysical perspective, everything being energy sounded pretty nice but hard to accept most of the time.

As science evolved, they discovered that if you take a chair and break it down to its most essential component you would end up with an atom. If you take a human organ and do the same you will also end up with an atom. And the same principle applies to any kind of physical form. What is interesting is that scientists also noticed that when you study different atoms, regardless of where they came from, they all share the *same* essential components. So an atom from a human eye was no different than an atom from a piece of wood or a flower or a rubber. That led to the conclusion that everything physical shares the *same* raw material. However, an atom is still matter. It's still something that can be seen, even if it's through a microscope.

Then a new ramification of science called Quantum Physics emerged. With the help of modern technology through the development of more sophisticated devices, Quantum physicists have managed to break down an atom as far as they could, only to find out that at its most primordial level, that which at one point was considered to be solid matter, was nothing more than empty space. That space quantum scientists refer to as a field of energy and information.

So everything being energy and God being one with everything, some scientists and almost all metaphysical teachers began to equate God with energy. Here is where it gets interesting. These same scientists who believe in a God or Higher Power are in agreement with metaphysical teachers by saying that God is eternal, never changing, without beginning and without ending.

Gary Renard, best-selling author of *The Disappearance of The Universe,* brought something to the surface which challenged this whole idea of God or Spirit being energy. According to science, although energy cannot be destroyed, it can be changed or transformed. That being the case, then the theory of God being energy cannot be true because how could that which is eternal, never changing, be changed or transformed? *A Course in Miracles* reminds me: "*Whatever is true is eternal, and cannot change or be changed. Spirit is therefore unalterable because it is already perfect...*" T-1.V.5:1-2

Imagine my frustration when my beliefs around energy were challenged. So in essence, who you are cannot be defined as either Spirit or energy. Who you are is something that *must be experienced*. But how can that be experienced you may ask? *By removing the blocks* to the awareness of *love's presence*. And what are these blocks? Simply put, all the *beliefs, concepts, notions* and *ideas* you have about yourself and the world in general. Having now a glimpse of what is involved in understanding what your True Self really is, let's move on to the remaining sentences of *A Course in Miracles'* introduction.

The opposite of love is fear, but what is all-encompassing can have no opposite.

This means that if love is all there is, or *oneness* if you rather think of it that way, then there could be *nothing else*. In other words, there could be *no* labels, *no* opposites. If love is all that there is, can you think of anything that love is not? You may say that anger is not love. Let me ask you again. If love is *all* that there is, can you think of *anything* that love is not? *The answer is no.* And yet most people would agree that anger exists because at some point or another, some more often than others have experienced angry feelings.

If love is all that there is, and some of us have experienced anger, where did that anger come from? Or who made up that anger? Only someone who *thinks* that he/she is not love could experience angry feelings. Simply said, you cannot not be, that which you already are. So you can convince yourself that you are not love in order to experience anger. But the experience of anger is not *Who you really are*. It is something *you made up* in order to *block* the awareness of love's presence, of your True Self. As you can see, operating from your false sense of self, your human identity, aside from having experiences that are incongruent with your true nature, such as experiencing hate or lack just to name a few, you also find yourself seeking, or wanting, all sorts experiences, not because they are not already a part of you, but because *you* have *forgotten* Who you really are.

That's why it is said: *"But **seek ye first the kingdom** of God, and his righteousness; and all these things shall be added unto you."* **[Matthew 6:33]** Where is the kingdom? *Within you!* Let's take a look at what most religions say in regards to the kingdom being within by reading the following excerpts from Jeffrey Moses' book titled *Oneness, Great Principles Shared by All Religions:*

Christianity: *"The Kingdom of God cometh not with observation: neither shall they say, Lo here! or lo there! for, behold, the kingdom of God is within you."*
Confucianism: *"What the undeveloped man seeks is outside; what the advanced man seeks is within himself."*
Buddhism: *"If you think the law is outside yourself, you are embracing not the absolute law but some inferior teaching."*
Shintoism: *"Do not search in distant skies for God. In man's own heart is He found."*

Hinduism: *"God bides hidden in the hearts of all."*
Sikhism: *"Why will thou go into the jungles? What do you hope to find there? Even as the scent dwells within the flower, so God within thine own heart ever abides. Seek Him with earnestness and find him there."*
Sufism: *"If human beings know their own inner secrets, they would never look elsewhere seeking for happiness and peace."*

And as far as seeking the Kingdom, The Course takes it one step further by saying; *"Instead of 'Seek ye first the Kingdom of Heaven' say, 'Will ye first the Kingdom of Heaven,' and you have said, 'I know what I am and I accept my own inheritance.'"* So in seeking or should we say, *willing* the kingdom of God, meaning looking within as opposed to without, your True Self *reveals* itself through you along with *everything* you have ever longed for and more. Be careful here because what you long for or more is far *beyond* what you could possibly imagine. Is *not of this world*. Joel S. Goldsmith in his book *The Infinite Way* wrote:

> *While we strive and struggle and contend with the so-called power of this world, combating sickness and sin or lack, spiritual sense reveals that 'My kingdom is not of this world.' Only as we* **transcend the desire to improve our humanhood** *do we understand this vital statement. When, however, we leave the realm of human betterment, we catch the first glimpse of the meaning of 'I have overcome the world.'"*

A Course in Miracles reminds me: *"The world I see holds nothing that I want. Beyond this world there is a world I want."* **W-**

pI.129.9:4-5 Do not let what I just said confuse you for it will become clear to you as you continue reading. So if *Who you really are* is not this body, then how is it possible that you cannot see or experience your True Self? It is because of what The Course refers to as the ego. The ego is nothing but a belief in separation. *A Course in Miracles* reminds me: *"The ego is idolatry; the sign of limited and separated self, born in a body, doomed to suffer and to end its life in death."* **W-pII.330.12.1:1** It is what is *projecting* the world that you see. As a matter of fact, it is what projected you. Therefore, you don't have en ego, *you are the ego!* But I will elaborate on this later on. Meanwhile, *A Course in Miracles* also reminds me: *"When you have been caught in the world of perception you are caught in a dream. You cannot escape without help, because **everything your senses show merely witnesses to the reality of the dream**."* Since a picture paints a thousand words, the following illustrations will assist you in better understanding the relation between your True Self and the ego.

> **Who You Are:**
> Love
> Infinite
> Abundant
> Perfect
> Whole
> Complete
> Joyous
> Happy
> Peace
> Omnipresent
> Omnipotent

These are not things or states you strive to achieve; these are your *True qualities*. These are your *natural states* of *Being*. They are all encompassing within Oneness. So you are *not* trying to become abundant because *you are* abundant. You don't need to search for love because *you are* love. You don't need to do anything in order to experience happiness because *you are* happiness. Nothing in your world needs to change in order for you to experience peace because *you are* peace. In other words, you *do not* need to create or attract or to change *anything*

> *The irony or paradox is, as you reveal through you, the qualities of your God Self, circumstances and conditions tend to automatically change.*

in the world in order for you to experience any of the qualities of God because in essence *you are God*. Below is what most religions say regarding man being created in the image and likeness of God according to author Jeffrey Moses' research, taken from his book titled *Oneness, Great principles Shared by All Religions:*

>**Judaism:** *"God created man in His own image, in the image of god created He him."*
>**Islam:** *"On God's own nature has been modeled man's."*
>**Sikhism:** *"O man, in God's image is he."*
>**Taoism:** *"The Supreme gives man His expression, and gives him His form."*
>**Christianity:** *"Know ye not that we are the temple of God, and that the Spirit of God dwelleth in you?"*
>**Bahá'í:** *"I created thee, have engraven on thee Mine image, and revealed to thee my Beauty."*

So to experience your *True* nature, all you need to do is remove the blocks that are not allowing you to have the direct experience of *Who you really are*. Since as within so is without, you find yourself having experiences that reflect back at you the qualities you are calling forth. Here is something you must understand. Calling forth the qualities of your True Self does not mean that your circumstances have to change. The only thing that is changing is the way you feel and see yourself in the midst of whatever is taking place in your life.

At this point you may be wondering that if someone knows, at least intellectually, who he or she truly is, why does that person continue to experience challenges? The following illustration will give you a better understanding as to why that seems to be the case for most people.

As you can see, it seems like the qualities of God, of *Who you are*, are not as clear as the ego, however they are still there. Maybe in the background but they are still there. The challenge is, the ego looks so much clearer than your true qualities that you have begun to convince yourself that what seems clear to you is true reality. *A Course in Miracles* reminds me: *"You do not doubt that the body's eyes can see. You do not doubt the images they show you are reality.* **Your faith lies in the darkness, not the light."** **W-pI.91.3:3-5**

> *You do not doubt that the body's eyes can see. You do not doubt the images they show you are reality. Your faith lies in the darkness, not the light.*

So when the idea of an ego was accepted as real, three things simultaneously took place. First, your God qualities became obscured by the presence of an ego that looks more convincing to you than your *true* Self. Second, a world filled with illusions has being projected, which gave birth to all your seeming problems. And third, because you believe that the world of illusion is real, your whole life is nothing but a problem-solving uphill battle with just a few moments of seeming happiness in between, as shown in the following illustration.

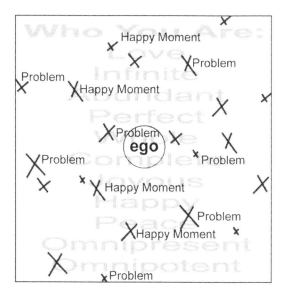

—Notice I said *seeming* happiness as opposed to *true* happiness. And that is because your seeming happiness is dependent on how the illusionary world you have made up behaves. For example, if there is money in the bank, you think you are happy. But what happens if someone takes it away? You would probably feel angry, fearful, depressed, sad and the list can go on. However, the ego does not stop there. Here is the other side of the coin, once you have the money you worked so hard to get, a *new* fear arises, the fear of *losing* it. Now you have to protect it, and from there greediness as well as all sorts of new worries and concerns are born. Mother Teresa once said: *"I come from a country where I have seen people having one banana and shared half, then I come to your country where I see people having plenty of bananas and do not even share one."* So no matter what, you can never experience *true* happiness and joy if you are operating from your ego. Same with everything you think is your source of happiness and joy.

Now that life is filled with all sorts of problems, let's see now how the world of illusion or the ego makes you believe that the more problems you solve, the more you expand by looking at the following illustration:

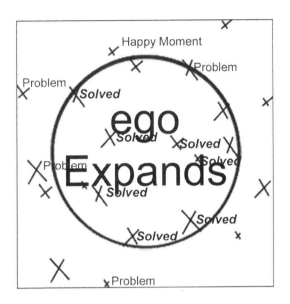

Now that you have temporarily forgotten *Who you really are*, many teachers proclaim that life is filled with problems, and that as you solve bigger and bigger problems you grow and expand. It is very *dangerous* to believe that problem solving is either a good thing or the natural way of life. I have even seen teachers, and well meaning by the way, who try to spiritualize the ego by implying that as you solve more problems you are expanding in consciousness. What they do not realize is, all you are doing is *pulling farther and farther away* from your True Self.

As you saw in the previous illustration, the bigger you become by solving problems, the qualities of your True Self are hidden further and further in the background, making it *almost impossible* for you to recognize them. Needless to say, they *are still there* and will *always* be there for they are *Who you really are*! At this point you may ask, *"What's necessary for me to bring forth my true qualities, especially while experiencing all these seeming problems?"* The answer is very *simple*. The question is, are you *ready* or *willing* to embrace the answer? Let's take a look at the following illustration before sharing how to bring forth the qualities of your True Self:

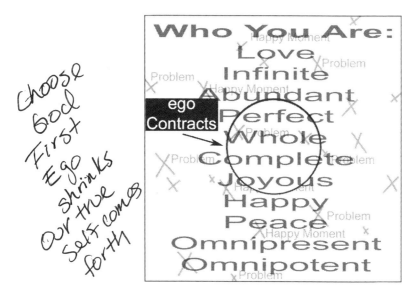

First, notice what happens when the ego gets smaller. On one hand all your "problems" cease to affect you while *simultaneously* your True Self *naturally* emerges. See how simple it is? That's why The Course reminds us that we have only one problem, and that is, we *forgot,* or I should say *I forgot* that God and I are One. In solving that *one* single problem, all the other seeming problems *automatically* disappear. Let's keep in mind however that in the world that we live in, we will experience problems for that is the nature of a world that is dual. But by not being affected by our "problems", we can deal with them more effectively.

> If the world we are seeing is considered to be an illusion, then by default it must not be real. It may appear to be so but the truth is, it is not.

So how do you go about shrinking the ego? In a nutshell, the way you shrink the ego is by choosing God *first*. The act of choosing God first is by simply choosing *peace* at all times. However there is more to this. So for now I have to ask you to trust that the answers will reveal themselves through you as you continue reading the content of this book since the ego is very complicated and I am still working on strengthening your foundation. Then you'll be doing the work that will lead you to the experience you are seeking as opposed to just having a theoretical understanding of Who you are.

Using myself as an example, right this moment I am trusting that if I keep my full awareness on God and not on any of the seeming challenges that are taking place in my life, trusting that everything is unfolding however it is supposed to, by maintaining my peace I will be guided as to what sort of action to take, *if needed,* at any given moment. That way anything that is *not* in alignment with my True self will *disappear* from my awareness enabling me to remember *Who I really am.* That would be the simple answer. But the ego being so insidious, we probably need to approach what I have just shared from different angles before you can truly embrace and put into practice what this book has to offer.

So the inquiring mind asks, *"If who I am has nothing to do with what I see, hear, touch, feel, then what is all this stuff I am seeing, touching, feeling? Why does the body I am in seem real to me?* The answer is because all that we see, hear, touch, smell and feel, which I'll elaborate more in the book, is nothing but an *illusion.* That's why the last few lines of The Course's introduction says:

This course can therefore be summarized up very simply in this way;

Nothing real can be threatened.
Pay close attention. If Who You are is *Real*, meaning that your True Self is non-physical, then nothing of this world could possibly threaten you.

Nothing unreal exists.
If the world we are seeing is considered to be an illusion, then by default it must not be real. It may appear to be so but the truth is, it is not. Therefore it must not exist. Here is how it works. This little part of you, this belief that we refer to as the ego, begins to project outward an illusionary world in the form of separate images, you being one of them. That's why the Course refers to us as *The "Hero" of the*

dream **T-27.VIII**. But for now, I have to keep the language dual as if there is a you who is projecting so that the content of this book can be easily understood and assimilated.

Continuing with this chapter's content, when you see those images, instead of you seeing them for what they really are, illusions, you react to them as if they are real. So by reacting to the illusions, you solidify them more in the screen of your conscious awareness. This becomes a never-ending cycle as shown in the illustration below:

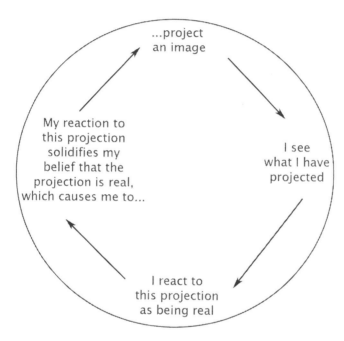

Herein lies the peace of God.

When you can see the world as what it is, just an illusion, where the images have no power over you, then you can be at peace no matter what your circumstances may look like. You can simply look right through them *without* having to *react* to them. That does not mean you are trying to change any illusion, you are simply not identifying yourself with them because you now know *Who you really are* as opposed to identifying yourself with your human experience. A Course in Miracles reminds me, *"But who reacts to figures in a dream unless he sees them as if they were real? The instant that he sees them as they are they have no more effects on him, because he understands he gave them their effects by causing them and making them seem real."* **T-27.VIII.4:4-5**

This raises all sorts of questions such as: *"But if I am not this body, then what's my reason for being here? What am I supposed to do while I live in this world that appears to be real to me? Can I live a normal life? Can I enjoy the things this world of illusion has to offer? Can I create what I want?"* And the list can go on forever. The answers to these questions and more will be revealed through you as you read the content of this book in the same way they were revealed through me.

So how can you reverse what you have made up? From *A Course in Miracles'* Workbook for students here is what I am reminded of. "*Your faith lies in the darkness, not the light. How can this be reversed? For you it is impossible, but you are not alone in this.*" What you see with your physical eyes is the illusion also known as your darkness. And because you see it, that's where your faith lies. The reason why you cannot reverse it by yourself is *because you cannot be your guide to miracles, for it is you who made them necessary."* **T-14.XI.7:1** So you need the One *outside* of the illusion to lead you out of it. You need ***the gift from God.***

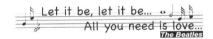

II
The Gift From God

"I said that I am with you always, even unto the end of the world. That is why I am the light of the world. If I am with you in the loneliness of the world, the loneliness is gone.
-A Course in Miracles [Text: chapter 8, section IV, paragraph 2, sentence 4]

"...and, lo, I am with you always, even unto the end of the world."
-Bible [Matthew: chapter 28, verse 20]

A *Course In Miracles* reminds me: "*A guide **does not control** but he does direct, leaving it up to you to follow.*" To help you better understand what the Gift from God is, let's take a look at this thing called "our oneness with God," because it will help to not only solidify this concept of the world being an illusion, it will also bring congruency to the chapters that follow. And by the way, I would like to clarify two things. One, even when The Course clearly states that God has no gender for God is pure Oneness it refers to God as Him. Having said that, feel free to replace the name God with one that resonates with you best. Keep in mind however that the name is *irrelevant*. The Tao reminds us; "*The Names that can be given are not absolute names. The Nameless is the origin of Heaven and Earth; the Named is the Mother of all things.*" In simpler words, the *Nameless*, being the origin of "Heaven" and "Earth" is God, which *can't* be named. The names are the *labels* we give to each individual *illusion*.

To begin elaborating on our oneness with God, I would like to share a line from The Course, which says, "*The recognition of God is the recognition of yourself. There is no separation of God and His creation.*" So if God is all that there is, then everything we see is a part of God. That means you, me, everyone and *everything* is God. However, since you are looking at the world through your physical eyes, in other words, the eyes of the ego, all the illusions that you see as separate simply reinforce your belief in separation. Therefore, if for example you see yourself as separate from me, what you are experiencing is your own separation from God through the illusion of seeing me apart from you. Interesting isn't it? So *Who you really are* is One with God, One Who's qualities are perfect love, infinite abundance, pure joy and happiness, permanent peace, meanwhile here you are experiencing duality such as good and evil, happy and sad, pleasure and pain, joy and sorrow and so on. That being the case, what you are having right here on earth through the experience of separation, is none other than the experience of *hell*. Hell, not because of the earth being "bad," for that would simply be a judgment, but because you are having an experience that is *opposite* of your *True* nature.

> *The recognition of God is the recognition of yourself. There is no separation of God and His creation.*

So in order to experience your oneness with God, all you need to do is make the *decision* to let go of the *belief that you are separate*. And for that you would need the help from a part of you that is not caught up in the illusion. And that is *the gift from God* also known as **The Holy Spirit**. If you recall from the previous chapter, *A Course in Miracles* reminds me: "*When you have been caught in the world of perception you are caught up in a dream.*

*You cannot escape without help, because **everything** your senses show merely **witnesses** to the reality of the **dream**."* **ACIM Preface** You may also recall the line from the Course that stated, *"You cannot be your guide to miracles, for it is you who made them necessary."* T-14.XI.6:7 Who or What is the Holy Spirit? It is the part of your mind that *remembers* your *True* nature, it is the mediator between your imagined ego-self and God, it is the One that is *always* communicating with you in the stillness. *A Course in Miracles* reminds me: *"God has provided the Answer, the only Way out, the true Helper. It is the function of His Voice, His Holy Spirit, to mediate between the two worlds. He can do this because, while on the one hand He knows the truth, on the other He also recognizes our illusions, but without believing in them."* **ACIM Preface** *A Course in Miracles* also reminds me *"The Holy Spirit is the Translator of the laws of God to those who do not understand them. You could not do this yourself because a conflicted mind cannot be faithful to one meaning, and will therefore change the meaning to preserve the form."* T-7.II.4:5-6 I am going to use an example about Jesus that although it is not true, it will help explain my point.

When Jesus was "living" among us, it was like having The Holy Spirit appear to them in the illusionary form of the body of a male. For our generation however, even when we may not have Jesus in physical form to help remind us of our *True* nature, the Holy Spirit is that inner voice, that inner presence that can lead us to our awakening, *only if* we are willing to *listen*. That's why The Course says: *"It is the Holy Spirit's goal **to help us escape** from the dream world by teaching us how to **reverse** our thinking **and unlearn** our mistakes."* **ACIM Preface**

I would like to use the following analogy to better explain what I have just shared. Imagine that you are in this beautiful mansion sleeping in the most gorgeous and spacious room. The bed is huge and comfortable. So you went to sleep and started to dream. Your pleasant dream all of a sudden turned into a nightmare. Your body is shaking and you are terrified. You dream that you are in a cave and that monsters are following you. At that moment you have *forgotten* that you are just *dreaming*. You are actually very *safe*, but to you, it seems as if you are in huge danger. That's why *A Course in Miracles* reminds me: *"You are at home in God, dreaming of exile but perfectly capable of awakening to reality."* **T-10.I.2:1**

The fact that you are safe has not changed. The fact that you are in the mansion has not changed. The fact that you are in this wonderful bed has not changed. Yet you are having a horrific experience that *seems* real to you. Now let's say your mother comes along and sees you are having a horrible dream. Very softly she whispers in your ear; *"Sweetheart, wake up. It's only a dream. Wake up sweetheart."* That's why *A Course in Miracles* reminds me: *"How can you wake children in a more kindly way than by a gentle Voice that will not frighten them, but will merely remind them that the night is over and the light has come?"* **T-6.V.2:1**

For the sake of this example, your dream is the physical world you perceive with your senses. Yet who made up the dream? *Yourself.* The challenge is that the dream is not being made up consciously. That's why even when you are the one making the whole thing up, it seems like you have no power to change it, not even to wake yourself up from it. Your mom being the one outside of the dream is playing the role of the Holy Spirit. She is trying to wake you up so you no longer have such a horrible experience and return to Reality. Notice she is waking you up *gradually* so you can get use to her voice first. That's why *A Course in Miracles* reminds me: *"If a light is suddenly turned on while someone is dreaming a fearful dream, he may initially interpret the light itself as part of his dream and be afraid of it. However, when he awakens, the light is correctly perceived as the release from the dream, which is then no longer accorded reality."* **T-2.I.4:6-7** And what is Reality? *Not* the dream, which seems to you that it is, but the huge room with the wonderful bed inside the mansion where everything you ever wanted and needed is available to you. <u>In other words, *the Kingdom of Heaven*; your *Real* home in God.</u>

Now I would like to take this moment and go back to where I said that the example about Jesus was not true. If it is all a dream, then the historical Jesus could not have existed either for if there's no world, then there is no Jerusalem, no history, no people, nothing! Having said that, there is nothing wrong with believing in Jesus and seeing him as our elder brother, guide or teacher. What matters is not whether he existed or not, but whether we are willing to listen to his teachings.

You may ask; *"I can see the Holy Spirit, I can see the dream as my ego's projection, but where is God?"* Well, in reality God is one with everything, but to use language you can relate to, God is the mansion with everything in it and the bed and the Holy Spirit and you; in other words, God is *everything* because there is *nothing* that God is not. So what is it that would need to take place in order for you to have a pleasant experience? You can either change the dream to a different one, which is what most people try to do, or you can wake up. Trying to exchange the dream for another one will simply lead you to more nightmares because that is the nature of the dream world. That is why the Course states, *"To change illusions is to make no change."* **T-22.II.2:4** That's how the ego operates. Waking up, on the other hand, would lead you to the *remembrance* of *Who you really are*. That's why Jesus said, *"But **seek ye first the kingdom** of God, and his righteousness..."* [**Matthew 6:33**]

But if I am peacefully at home in God you may ask, then what's the purpose in dealing with the world of illusions (physical world) that according to most scriptures and spiritual teachers, was created by God? The answer lies in a very subtle but very disturbing technicality. And that is, ***God did not create the world that we see.***

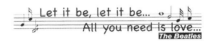

III
God Did Not Create The World That We See

"This world is not the Will of God, and so it is not real. Yet those who think it real must still believe there is another will, and one that leads to opposite effects from those He wills."
-A Course in Miracles [Workbook: lesson 166, paragraph 2, sentence 2]

"Love not the world, neither the things that are in the world. If any man love the world, the love of the Father is not in him."
-Bible [1 John: chapter 2, verse 15]

Now that you have a better understanding of what the ego is, the Holy Spirit and the illusionary nature of this world, let's explore this idea about God creating the world. *A Course in Miracles* reminds me: *"The world was made as an attack on God. It symbolizes fear. And what is fear except love's absence? Thus* the world was meant to be a place where God could enter not, and where His Son could be apart from Him." **W-pII.240.3.2:1-4** What *the scriptures* have to say in regard to the "creation" of the world is that *in the beginning* God created Heaven and earth, otherwise known as the physical world. Notice however that the scriptures say *in the beginning*.

Before I elaborate on this "in the beginning," notice that the Scriptures were not written by Jesus. As a matter of fact, if you go straight to the teachings of Jesus the Christ, the Bible could be reduced to maybe few pages. For example Genesis 1, versus 1 - 18, states:

1: *In the beginning God created the Heaven and the earth.*
2: *And the earth was without form, and void; and darkness was upon the face of the deep. And the Spirit of God moved upon the face of the waters.*

This suggests that in Oneness, which is your natural state, darkness is all that there was. Who wrote that? Definitely someone who has never experienced Oneness and made up his own concept of what anything other than the earth would be like.

3: *And God said, Let there be light: and there was light.*

Now we begin to experience opposites, for without light there is no darkness.

4: *And God saw the light, that it was good: and God divided the light from the darkness.*

Now aside from opposites, judgment is introduced by suggesting that one thing is good as opposed to bad.

5: *And God called the light Day, and the darkness he called Night. And the evening and the morning were the first day.*

The judgment continues as now we start labeling and naming things on this earth. At this point the illusion of time is being introduced by suggesting there is a first day.

> 6: *And God said, Let there be a firmament in the midst of the waters, and let it divide the waters from the waters.*

And the division and separation continues as you will continue to read in the lines that follow.

> 7: *And God made the firmament, and divided the waters which were under the firmament from the waters which were above the firmament: and it was so.*
> 8: *And God called the firmament Heaven. And the evening and the morning were the second day.*
> 9: *And God said, Let the waters under the heaven be gathered together unto one place, and let the dry land appear: and it was so.*
> 10: *And God called the dry land Earth; and the gathering together of the waters called he Seas: and God saw that it was good.*
> 11: *And God said, Let the earth bring forth grass, the herb yielding seed, and the fruit tree yielding fruit after his kind, whose seed is in itself, upon the earth: and it was so.*
> 12: *And the earth brought forth grass, and herb yielding seed after his kind, and the tree yielding fruit, whose seed was in itself, after his kind: and God saw that it was good.*
> 13: *And the evening and the morning were the third day.*

The illusion of time and space continue to be perpetuated.

> 14: *And God said, Let there be lights in the firmament of the heaven to divide the day from the night; and let them be for signs, and for seasons, and for days, and years:*

We have more division, and subdivision.

> 15: *And let them be for lights in the firmament of the heaven to give light upon the earth: and it was so.*
> 16: *And God made two great lights; the greater light to rule the day, and the lesser light to rule the night:* he made the stars also.

Now we not only have separation and judgment, but we are being introduced to a *hierarchy* of judgment by suggesting that one light is better than another.

> 17: *And God set them in the firmament of the Heaven to give light upon the earth,*
> 18: *And to rule over the day and over the night, and to divide the light from the darkness: and God saw that it was good.*

In addition to all the seeming judgment and separation created by "god", God is also seen as some kind of a distant ruler, looking upon something that seem to be outside of God.

Notice that none of what is being said in Genesis was attributed to Jesus. According to Genesis all of that was attributed to God. My question is, did God say these words or did the writers of the Scriptures make up what God said?

Now let's take a look at what Jesus has to say about the world and oneness. *"Love not the world, neither the things that are in the world. If any man love the world, the love of the Father is not in him."* [John 2:15] Interesting isn't? He is trying to keep our attention out of the world. Let's review what Jesus says through the gospel according to John, chapter 17:

> 13: *And now come I to thee; and these things I speak in the world, that they might have my joy fulfilled in themselves.*
> 14: *I have given them thy word; and the world hath hated them, because they are not of the world, even as I am not of the world.*
> 15: *I pray not that thou shouldest take them out of the world, but that thou shouldest keep them from the evil.*
> 16: *They are not of the world, even as I am not of the world.*
> 17: *Sanctify them through thy truth: thy word is truth.*

So far He is addressing the fact that what He speaks about and Who we really are is *not of this world*. Jesus is teaching us here that our True Self is *not* of this world. Understandably, this concept may seem difficult to anyone who perceives him or herself to be only a physical body living within a limited world. Consequently, if we choose to understand Jesus' teaching, we first may need to detach ourselves from our worldly and bodily perceptions. The words He speaks we need to hear them with ears that are *congruent* with *truth*, with a mindset that, once again, is *not of this world*. And to do so we *must* set aside *all* intellectual understanding because God *cannot* be understood intellectually. God has to be *experienced*.

> 18: *As thou hast sent me into the world, even so have I also sent them into the world.*
> 19: *And for their sakes I sanctify myself, that they also might be sanctified through the truth.*

The truth being that we are all one, if one is sanctified through truth, the rest most be sanctified as well.

> 20: *Neither pray I for these alone, but for them also which shall believe on me through their word;*
> 21: *That they all may be one; as thou, Father, art in me, and I in thee, that they also may be one in us: that the world may believe that thou hast sent me.*

Notice how Jesus speaks of the Father and the Son being one. The words "*Father, art in me, and I in thee*" states clearly that we are One as well as the verses that follow.

> 22: *And the glory which thou gavest me I have given them; that they may be one, even as we are one;*

> 23: *I in them, and thou in me, that they may be made perfect in one; and that the world may know that thou hast sent me, and hast loved them, as thou hast loved me.*
> 24: *Father, I will that they also, whom thou hast given me, be with me where I am; that they may behold my glory, which thou hast given me: for thou lovedst me before the foundation of the world.*
> 25: *O righteous Father, **the world hath not known thee: but I have known thee**, and these have known that thou hast sent me.*

Pay close attention to what you just read. When Jesus says: *"O righteous Father, the world hath not known thee:"* I want you to imagine Christopher Columbus before sailing onto uncharted waters. Those who didn't know that the world was round told him that there was an edge at the end of the horizon. And that if he embarked on that journey he would eventually fall off the edge of the earth. That would be the equivalent of those who wrote the Bible. Not being able to experience Heaven while perceiving themselves as limited, the writers of the Bible could not begin to conceive the True nature of God, yet they find themselves writing about what they suggest God said or did.

So Christopher Columbus embarked on his journey and discovered, not only that there was no edge at the end of the earth, but also that there are other lands at the opposite side of the globe. And yes, I know he found North America by mistake as opposed to what he was looking for which was India, but my point is, because he has traveled around the globe, he was able to report what he has discovered. Jesus, being the part of the mind that represent Truth, has actually *experienced* His oneness with the Father therefore He is then able to share with us His experience, not only through words, but through *example*, just so that we can follow. So the question is, whose teachings do you want to follow? The teachings of Jesus who experienced Truth, or do you rather follow the teachings of the ones who have *never* had the *direct experience* of being One with the Father?

> *The world as you perceive it cannot have been created by the Father, for the world is not as you see it. God creates only eternal and everything you see is perishable.*

So be mindful not to confuse what the Bible says with the teachings of Jesus the Christ because they are *two completely different books*. Once I heard a minister say: *"I practice the teachings of Jesus the Christ, not necessarily Christianity as it is taught."* Remember, that same Bible is the one that fundamentalist Christians use to promote separation and bigotry. It is the same Bible that religions use to promote guilt and fear of God. It is the same Bible that spiritualist and metaphysicians use to promote love and oneness, and it is the same Bible that the Ku Klux Klan uses to promote hatred and racism. Let's elaborate now on this "in the beginning."

Any spiritual teacher or teaching that equates the word beginning and/or ending with God, must assume that God is limited by boundaries of space and time. For without space and time there could be no beginning and no ending. So if God is eternal, then *before* the beginning there was God, and that's all there was, is, and will be. That's why *A Course in Miracles* reminds me: "*There are no beginnings and no endings in God, Whose universe is Himself.*" T-11.I.2:3

Now, if it is true that God is eternal, and we are created in the image and likeness of God, which means *without* beginning and *without* ending, then the heaven and earth we see with the physical eye *must not* have been one of God's creations because everything we see in the realm of the physical has a beginning and an ending. There is birth and death, the beginning of youth and the ending of it. We have transitory things that we acquire that we have no control over how long they will last. *A Course in Miracles* reminds me: "*The world as you perceive it cannot have been created by the Father, for the world is not as you see it. God creates **only** eternal and everything you see is perishable.*" **T-11.VII.1:1-2**

I would like to take it one step further. If the world in which God lives in is nothing but love and the world of our experience seems to be driven by fear, it would be a clear sign that this world could not be God's creation. And yes, it could be argued that God created a perfect world and because man was given freewill he is destroying it. Part III of this book addresses freewill by answering the question, "*I am confused about the concept of free will. Do I have free will or not?*" Before reading the answer I would *strongly* suggest you continue reading as opposed to getting sidetracked with questions and answers that may generate some degree of confusion until your foundation is solid.

A Course in Miracles reminds me: "*What if you recognize this world is an hallucination? What if you understood you made it up? What if you realized that those who seem to walk about in it, to sin and die, attack and murder and destroy themselves, are wholly unreal? Could you have faith in what you see, if you accepted this? And would you see it?*" **T.20.VIII.7:3-7** "*Hallucinations disappear when they are* *recognized for what they are. This is the healing and the remedy. Believe them not and they are gone.*" T.20.VIII.8:1-3

So if in order to stop all this suffering and pain, all you need to do is to wake up from this dream, why does it seem so difficult to do so? Because the ego being so clever, it has managed to convince you that in order for you to have a pleasant experience all you need to do is to exchange the dream for a more pleasant one. It had to, not because the ego knows better but because since the ego *is* the creator of the dream, i.e., the world that you see, the little "i" that thinks it is here, the moment you awaken the ego *dies*.

> *What if you recognize this world is an hallucination? What if you understood you made it up? What if you realized that those who seem to walk about in it, to sin and die, attack and murder and destroy themselves, are wholly unreal?*

So the ego, fearing death, will do *whatever it takes* to strike a bargain with you. It will promise you very short-lived pleasant experiences within the dream just to keep you from awakening to your *Real Self*. What you don't realize is that within the realm of the ego, all you may ever have are moments of pseudo-happiness followed by *continuous* pain and suffering. Because of the unconscious choice of bargaining with the ego by listening to its loud persuasive voice as opposed to the subtle peaceful one of the Holy Spirit, something had to be made up in order to attempt to escape from the never-ending pain and suffering only an ego-manufactured world could produce. That led to **the birth of false idols.**

♪ Let it be, let it be... ♫ ♪♪
All you need is love...
The Beatles

IV
The Birth of False Idols

"You cannot be faithful to two masters who ask conflicting things of you. What you use in fantasy you deny to truth. Yet what you give to truth to use for you is safe from fantasy."
-A Course in Miracles [Text: chapter 17, section I, paragraph 2, sentence 4, 5]

"No man can serve two masters: for either he will hate the one, and love the other; or else he will hold to the one, and despise the other. Ye cannot serve God and mammon."
-Bible [Matthew: chapter 6, verse 24]

A *Course In Miracles* reminds me: "All idols of this world were made to keep the truth within **from being known to you**, and to maintain allegiance to the dream that you must find what is outside yourself to be complete and happy. It is vain to worship idols in the hope of peace. God dwells within, and your completion lies in

Him. No idol takes His place. Look not to idols. ***Do not seek outside yourself."***

Although when employing the term false idols, The Course is referring to anything we are attached to or give importance to in this illusory world of physical form, I am going to use it to address anyone who considers himself or herself to be a bringer of truth or I should say claim to have any answers. That being said, if I am writing this book, where do I fit in this? Am I a teacher, a spiritual guide, a mentor, a coach? Truthfully, none of these titles. In fact, no title should be ascribed to me based on the knowledge and information shared by me through this book. Consider me not as you would a false idol, one with all your answers, consider and remember me as someone here to remind you that all the answers you are seeking can *only* be found within. And that *only* the Holy Spirit can lead you to *Truth*.

I am just like a different kind of referee, one that when you feel tempted to step out of the game, although I will not attempt to force you back in the game for that would be interfering with your own process, I would gently suggest for you to get back on the court so that the Holy Spirit can continue doing the work through you; the work you have chosen to do at your current level of readiness. This is the purpose I fill in my illusionary role for you. If you see me as someone who has any answers, I am considered a *false idol*.

If you are not ready to do your work, the support that you need will not be recognized within the field of your conscious awareness. Every book I have ever read and every teacher I have studied with were always there to lead me to the next stage on this path. I was simply not able to recognize their existence, because at the time I wasn't ready. To give you an example, when I was introduced to *A Course in Miracles*, I was not ready for its teachings. Many years later, here I am, an avid student of The Course.

> *If you are not ready to do your work, the support that you need will not be recognized within the field of your conscious awareness.*

Even when most of what I have written is based on my experiences as I practice the teachings of The Course, as I said near the beginning of this book, what attracted me to these teachings, is the fact that I was led to answers *without* giving me *specific* answers. Actually there is only *one* answer, but continue reading, you'll be led to it. In other words, the answer that was already within began to surface as I started *practicing* letting go and trusting. *A Course in Miracles* reminds me: "*Simply do this: Be still, and lay aside all thoughts of what you are and what God is; all concepts you have learned about the world; all images you hold about yourself. Empty your mind of everything it thinks is either true or false, or good or bad, of every thought it judges worthy, and all the ideas of which it is ashamed.* **Hold onto nothing,** *Do not bring with you one thought the past has taught, nor one belief you ever learned before from anything. Forget this world,* **forget this course***, and come with wholly empty hands unto your God.*" **W-pI.189.7:1-5**

With that said, before diving deeper into this chapter, there is something I want you to understand. I don't consider false idols as being negative. As a matter of fact, had it not been for them many of us would not have been drawn to a deeper understanding of our True Self. In other words, I see them as vehicles that can help force people to move in the right direction, *not* by teaching them who they are but by showing them who they are *not*. In simple terms, by finding out that what they teach does not work, forces us to look somewhere else, *within*!

So what would give rise to false idols? In my opinion I would say one thing disguised as two. One, the ego's plan for its survival, and two, our deep yearning to help others, which is also another tactic employed by the ego for its survival. Let's elaborate on each so you can better understand my point.

The Ego's Plan for Its Survival

A powerful tactic of the Ego is to project a world of illusions, where we keep looking for answers and solutions to all our problems outside ourselves, out in the world, where they can never be found. Looking up to false idols, like technology, information, teachers, gurus and so on, although they may serve a temporary purpose, cannot lead us to truth since they are part of the illusion. The reason being, as Gary Renard once said, is because it is like asking the illusion to lead us out of the illusion. All that the ego can do, and it will if we let it, is keep us trapped within the illusion, which places us on a perpetual rollercoaster ride between pain and pleasure. Let's now take a look at the second reason for the birth of false idols.

Our Deep Yearning For Helping Others

Even when it could be argued that there are people who are very blinded by their darkness and that there is no way they could feel for anyone, I would say that even if for a split second, there is a part deep within that feels hurt when someone else hurts. And that is because, even when we may try to deny it, the fact remains that we are all one. I will also add that at the core of our being, our True nature calls for helping others, not for the reasons you may have been taught, such as the old story I am about to share, but because of something that will become very clear to you as you read the rest of this book. I would like to share an old story about a great master sitting by the edge of a river.

> *"A monk was sitting by the edge of a river when all of a sudden he sees a scorpion falling into the water. The monk reached out to save the scorpion, only to be stung by it. The scorpion fell again into the water and the monk reached out for the second time, only to be stung by the scorpion again. Once again the scorpion fell into the water, and as the monk reached out to save him, an observer asked the monk; 'Excuse me, but why do you keep reaching out to such an ungrateful creature when all it does is sting you every time you save it?' The monk replied, 'Because the purpose of the scorpion is to sting, but the purpose of the human being is to save.'"*

So out of our deep yearning to serve, and help others, the ego found another way to stay alive. It made us believe that we have all the answers and therefore can alleviate others' seeming pain. This gives the ego a false sense of power, of superiority, which in turn makes us feel good. (Once again, keep in mind however that there are no others, which brings us back to the first ego trap, the illusion of an outside world, a world filled with separation). For the sake of keeping the continuity of what is being shared about the ego's yearn for helping others, using myself as an example, when I started my journey and began to read more about success, spirituality, healing, metaphysics, and everything else in between, something within moved me to share everything I was learning for the sole purpose of helping others.

I got such a sense of gratitude and fulfillment when I put a smile on someone's face or if I could help someone believe in themselves a bit more. It reminded me of Ralph Waldo Emerson when he said, *"To know that one life has breathed easier because you have lived, that is to have succeeded."* But as I continued to participate in seminars and listening to all these teachers, something within could not resonate. It was as if somewhere deep within my being, part of me knew that there was more to what I was being taught. And that is because the part of me that wanted to help others through processes and techniques I've learned throughout the years, was the ego disguised as a savior.

Then the time came when I began to doubt myself. I started to wonder if what I was learning was actually true. I began to have experiences that would defy logic. I noticed that the tools given and the principles taught by all these well-meaning teachers were not really consistent, not to mention how many of them made their living not by example but by manipulating people with fear-based marketing tactics. I found myself doing the same thing for a while. Then I came to a place where I no longer felt that I had to manipulate others.

As I deepened my work, I started to learn how to differentiate between the voice of the ego and the Voice of the Holy Spirit. So even when a deep yearning to help others gave birth to false idols, I came to realize that if I am operating from ego, it is impossible to lead others to Truth, not that I could anyway, but because the ego does not know Truth. In other words, if the ego does not know how to love, how could someone coming from that place teach others True love, even when they have the best intentions like most of us have? That's why *A Course in Miracles*' reminds me: "*Trust not your good intentions. They are not enough.*" T-18.IV.2:1-2

Mahatma Gandhi once said; "**Be the change you want to see in the world**." Also *A Course in Miracles* manual for teachers reminds me: "*Peace is **impossible** to those who look on war. Peace is **inevitable** to those who **offer** it.*" Notice it did not say to those who teach about it or to those who talk about it but to those who *offer* it, because in order to offer it you have to *be* it. Get it? How can I teach peace if deep within I am not peaceful, yet expect others to be at peace? There is no difference between a terrorist and an activist when they *both* come from a place of *fear, righteousness,* and *judgment*. A true peacemaker *radiates* peace instead of preaching about it.

Yes, the ego can disguise itself as a victim, as well as a savior, in order to keep us trapped within the illusion called the physical realm. In this chapter, I will share some of the most popular ideas and concepts taught by so many, so you can see the difference between what could be considered the ego's point of view versus the Holy Spirit's. I am not asking you to believe anything I say, I am simply asking you to be open and to listen to *your* inner voice. If something resonates as true, you'll know. The Course says that spirituality is very simple but the ego is very complicated. That being the case, many statements may seem repetitive, as I elaborate on each concept, belief and/or idea.

> *...the ego can disguise itself as a victim, as well as a savior, in order to keep us trapped within the illusion called the physical realm.*

Also remember that the comparisons presented here are simply observations. I have met teachers who are the most kind, loving, amazing individuals in the spiritual and business field and I know in my heart they have the best intentions. But having great intentions does not mean that the information is accurate. *A Course in Miracles* reminds me: *"There are two teachers only, who point in different ways. And you will go along the way your chosen teacher leads. There are but two directions you can take, while time remains and choice is meaningful. For never will another road be made except the way to Heaven. You but choose whether to go towards Heaven* (by listening to the Holy Spirit's Voice) *or away to nowhere* (by listening to the ego). *There is nothing else to choose."* **T-26.V.1:7-12**

The reason why the information being taught by most teachers is not necessarily accurate is because most of them are operating from beliefs and *beliefs* can be changed. So if a belief can be changed, then by nature it *cannot* be true. Remember that a belief is a concept, an idea, something we made up in order to give validity to our experience. That being the case, a belief is a lie regardless of what our physical senses perceive as true. Truth on the other hand is consistent, never-changing, like God, it is not evolving or expanding, it just is!

That's why *A Course in Miracles* reminds me: *"Truth is the absence of illusion; illusion the absence of truth. Both cannot be together, nor perceived in the same place."* **T-19.I.5:8-9** Could you imagine what it would be like if God kept changing?

One final reminder before moving on. I am using language you can relate to while addressing each topic, knowing that there is no "they" nor "us" just only One as I have mentioned before. So this chapter is dual in content for the objective is to begin doubting all that we have been taught. That's why we must keep in mind that our main intention is to wake up from this dream, to remember that this world does not exist, and it is not about trying to achieve a particular thing.

That does not mean you cannot have an incredible experience while having this human experience. As a matter of fact, the more you let go and trust, that's the kind of experience you open yourself up to, which you'll understand why as you read further because that kind of experience takes place through a change in perception not an exchange of illusions. I will address now some of the most popular ideas and concepts being taught in the world of contemporary spirituality and self help.

Most Predominant Beliefs, i.e. Illusions

Visualization

The purpose of visualization supposedly is for us to manifest something we desire in our lives. But why would we want to manifest anything in particular? Because at some level we believe that whatever it is we manifest is going to bring us happiness or is going to fill in a void.

For example some may say, "If I have more money I would be happy or I can do more things or if I was in a relationship I would feel loved or if I had this house or that thing I would be satisfied." And the list can go on forever. Now let me ask you, who is the one that *needs* to manifest anything in order to feel happy or loved or abundant and so on? The answer is, the ego, the part of you who *thinks* that it is disconnected from the *Real* Source, the one who has *forgotten Who you are*, which is nothing less than an extension of God.

Visualizing whatever it is you think you need or want is a very powerful tactic that the ego employs to not only keep you from being in the present, which I will address in more detail later, but also to keep you from focusing your attention within. As long as you keep looking out for whatever you think is missing, you won't be able to recognize your *natural inheritance*, which is nothing less than the kingdom of God. And where is the kingdom of God? *Within you!* As I shared earlier in the book, the scriptures say; *"Neither shall they say, Lo here! or, lo there! for, behold, the kingdom of God is within you."* [Luke:17:21] And once again, but this time using a different passage from The Course, it takes it one step further by saying that *you are* the kingdom. *A Course in Miracles* reminds me: **"Because you are the Kingdom of God** *I can lead you back to your own creations. You do not recognize them now, but what has been dissociated* **is still there."** T-4.VI.7:7-8

Now, what is it that the ego is trying to do at any cost? The ego is trying to stay alive. So, if visualizing is one of many means for getting whatever it is you want, and you get it, not only then survival of the ego is assured but there is also another challenge. And that is that according to The Course, the ego's mantra is *seek and never find*. So even if you end up getting whatever it is you want, sooner or later, that which you have manifested from that place of fear (illusion of separation) is going to bring some kind of suffering. So, while you get the million dollars, for example, something else you cherish is lost or even that which you thought you wanted ends up being your greatest nightmare.

I would like to share an example. I have a friend who writes what he wants and sets out to get it. One day he decided he wanted to have a wife and kids, to start a family. He read books, and went out to find someone he felt compatible with. When he did, everything seemed to be going well until they got married. Long story short, the divorce and the nightmare that he experienced was something I would not want to wish to anyone. Bottom line is, whatever it is you are looking for out there is *never* going to bring you peace. Your experience may not be as extreme as his, but you set yourself up to those kinds of experiences whenever you try to tell God your plans. All I am saying is, there is a much *simpler* way, if you are *open* and *ready*.

So what happens when we let go and let God? An interesting thing takes place. Visualization is replaced by *visioning*. The visioning process is completely opposite of visualization for it is *not* about coming up with images of what we want, but allowing the images to *naturally* appear on the screen of our conscious awareness. Simply put, you don't ask God for what you want; you simply make yourself available so that God can use you. And the process is not only easier it is actually *natural*. Even though most people think that by visualizing what they want, what they are doing is asking God for help, or as some may say, "co-creating" with God, in reality, what they are saying is; *"God please let me do this on my own."* So we visualize what we want, put lots of energy into it and realize that we end up exhausted because it does not seem natural. And the truth is, it is *not* natural because of the following paradox which says, *"At the same time that you are the producer, the director and the writer of your own movie, at that very same time you play an extra in a much bigger play."* So even when you think you are the one making choices, at a much deeper level these are choices you are being moved to make, as denoted in the saying, *God's Will be done.*

That being said, why is it that we want to be led by visioning as opposed to visualization? Because we want to get out of our way, so we can wake up from this dream in which we find ourselves. *A Course in Miracles* reminds me: *"Vision is the means by which the Holy Spirit translates your nightmares into happy dreams; your wild hallucinations that show you all the fearful outcomes of imagined sin into the calm and reassuring sights with which He would replace them."* **T-20.VIII.10:4**

What The Course refers to as the *happy dream* is just correction of perception, which I'll talk about it later. But for now, I would like to share a personal story which I think you'll enjoy: Around 1994, I had this desire to move to California; it was not really a goal, but more like a calling. Henceforth, I mysteriously began to draw all kinds of opportunities to fulfill that desire. However, the challenge was choosing the right time.

Before moving forward with the story, I want you to notice something. Although it seemed is if I was visualizing what I thought I wanted, the reality was that these images of me being in California *just kept filling up my consciousness.* So it wasn't that I was trying to visualize something, I was being presented with these images *without me having to do anything*.

47

So how did I end up in California my first time? Out of the blue, 20th Century Fox Television contacted me and offered me a development deal for a television sitcom for which I would receive the amount of $30,000 to move to California. It all came to me *without any effort* on my part. What do you mean without any effort on my part, you may ask?

Well, after returning home from a comedy tour, there was a message on my answering machine from an agent out of West Palm Beach, Florida, who informed me how it all came about. 20th Century Fox Television was asking agents all over the United States to send tapes from comedians/actors that may fit the part for a project they had in mind. This particular agent was not representing me, but only knew me from when I worked at her club and taped a show there, which happened to be the tape she sent. She did not even ask for a commission. She sent the tape along with tapes of other comedians she had in mind. *All of this happened without me knowing about it.* Out of many submissions received from all over the United States, I was chosen and placed in a contract before they even met me. So by the time I arrived in California, I was handed a check. Notice how everything was arranged for me by the Holy Spirit, while all I did was make myself available for the vision to take form, and it all happened *easily* and *effortlessly*.

Once you accept His plan as the one function that you would fulfill, there will be nothing else the Holy Spirit will arrange for you without your effort.

A Course in Miracles reminds me: "*Once you accept His plan as the one function that you would fulfill, there will be nothing else the Holy Spirit will not arrange for you without your effort. He will go before you making straight your path, and leaving in your way no stones to trip on, and no obstacles to bar your way. Nothing you need will be denied. Not one seeming difficulty but will melt away before you reach it.*" **T-20.IV.8:4-7** I would like to clarify something. You probably thought that the experience of moving to California is what The Course talks about when you read the line ...*He will go before you making straight your path, and leaving in your way no stones to trip on,...* The Course is *not* referring to specific goals or things of this world that I may want to go after, but towards awakening. I just used the example of moving to California for entertainment purposes. In a later chapter I will elaborate more what The Course refers to as the happy dream.

One last thing I would like to add in regard to visioning. It is being taught by some teachers that visioning is something you deliberately set out to do. Like for example, someone would say, "I would like to create XYZ, so let's do a visioning to see what comes up." Well, that's like visualization because even when I am being open to images, I am still holding some degree of *expectation*, since I already have an idea in mind as to what I am visioning for. If visioning is viewed in that sense, you could say that it is another ego's tactic to help distract us from seeing the world as an illusion. Remember that if the world disappears, the ego disappears also. Since the ego may not be able to appeal to the spiritual community using conventional language, in other words "non-believers'" language, it has to come up with a plan to ensure its own survival. That being the case, giving the world spiritual attributes by saying that God created the world that we perceive with our physical senses for example, it helps keep spiritual seeker's attention out into the world (illusion), making it seem real, resulting in the ego's life being preserved.

But regardless of what you call it, visioning, brainstorming, etc., that's perfectly okay because words are meaningless. It is that from *my* understanding of The Course, the word vision is used as a way compare the way the Holy Sprit looks at the world as opposed to the ego. We must remember that the ego sees the world. The Holy Spirit sees the *Truth*! That's why *A Course in Miracles* reminds me: *"Vision would not be necessary had judgment not been made."* **T-20.VIII.1:5** Judgment is what we see with our eyes, which is the world. Remember, visioning on the other hand sees Truth, which is *not of this world*.

I just want you to understand that I am not implying that because I am writing this book that means I am visioning. What I am saying is, that as I make myself available to Truth, the images that come to mind are always in alignment with whatever it is I need to do next. And the goal is to awaken, not what to do in the world. But as of this moment, typing this manuscript is what I feel inspired to do. And the trip to California along with all the experiences I've had, and continue to have have no intrinsic value, they are transitory like everything else of this world. So as far as I am concerned, the *only* vision worth holding is that of the kingdom. Everything else is just specifics. And specifics are what keep us away from what the real goal is, which is God!

Goal Setting

Goal-setting, being a part of the illusion could also be referred to as fantasy. *A Course in Miracles* reminds me: *"Fantasy is an attempt to control reality according to false needs."* **T-1.VII.3:4** Also A Course in Miracles reminds me: *"The mind engaged in planning for itself is occupied in setting up control of future happenings. It does not think that it will be provided for, unless it makes its own provisions. Time becomes a future emphasis, to be controlled by learning and experience obtained from past events and previous beliefs. It overlooks the present; for it rests on the idea the past has taught enough to let the mind direct its future course."* **W-pI.135.15:1-4** That does not mean that there is anything wrong with planning. There is necessary planning in order to function in this world. But this is not what we are talking about here.

You could say that goal-setting is another form of visualization. The difference is goal-setting usually involves deadlines and a specific time frame as someone once said; *goals are dreams with a deadline.* Although, a vision in and of itself could be considered a goal, keeping your attention on the goal or target takes you out of the present moment awareness, which is the *only* time you are communicating with your True Self. There is an old paradox that says, *"When your mind is in the outcome, you are no longer in the process, but when your mind is in the process, the outcome is guaranteed."* What I invite you to notice is that it does not say *your* outcome but *the* outcome.

Because as you are led by your True Self, you will be led to "goals" that are in alignment with your *true* purpose, which is to awaken from the dream. That's how you can experience true joy and fulfillment. Remember that when your ego sets a goal, it comes from a place of fear, attachment and neediness. However, there is a difference between setting a goal and having a *sense of direction*. With the writing of this manuscript, I have a sense of direction. However, I am not attached to the outcome. I am just allowing and being in the process, knowing that it will lead to wherever it leads.

That's how I can experience peace of mind while most of the world is so busy *doing, doing, doing*. I experience *real* fulfillment, not because I am writing this book, but because there is a bigger plan behind the writing of this book and I am trusting in it. In spite of the fact that I may not be the best writer or speller, all I am doing is saying *yes* to my Self.

As a result of my willingness to *trust*, I am neither worried about my future nor concerned about any goals (fantasies), of which I have none, by the way. What I have is the knowledge of my Real Source and Supply; hence, knowing that all I need is provided. Remember that the unfoldment of your life is not so you can accomplish your goals, but so that you can remember *Who you really are*. Just like visualization, goal setting is another way of keeping your attention out there, which is all the ego is trying to do.

Developing a Plan of Action

Why would you need to make plans? From the ego's point of view, it would be because of safety reasons. If the ego is all about control, imagine what it would be like to live a life *without* specific agendas or lack of control. *A Course in Miracles* reminds me: "*If there are plans to make, **you will be told of them**. They may not be the plans you thought were needed, nor indeed the answers to the problems which you thought confronted you. But they are answers to another kind of question, which remains unanswered yet in need of answering **until the Answer comes to** you at last.*" **W-pI.135.23:2-4**

A plan of action created from a peace of mind perspective, turns into a *vision* that evolves through *spontaneous right action.* Clearly stated, when you are in the moment , you make decisions that are *appropriate* for *that* specific situation, and spontaneous of course, meaning *without* premeditation. Therefore going with the flow can *never* be experienced by trying to figure things out in advance because you are not trying to control the outcome or attempting to run your life, you are simply *listening* to your own guidance while being *open* to the possibility of change. And yes, you may be guided from within to set up a specific plan of action for your business, project(s) or idea(s) and your life.

In other words, use common sense, for in this world, as I said before, plans are part of being able to function here. But do not attach yourself to them as important, nor as a source of security. Simply see them for what they are, remembering that in this world, nothing is meant to function, it is meant to simply distract us from keeping our attention on what is really important, peace of mind. If anything, plan your life accordingly so that you always make time for communing with your Self in silence.

God Helps Those Who Help Themselves

The truthfulness of this statement is based on its relativity. If you are operating from the ego-mind, the assumption here is that you tell God what you want and use God as your helper, so to speak. So, if you work hard at getting whatever it is you want (helping yourself) then God will help you achieve your plan. The deception or illusion lies in knowing what we want, because the ego is never satisfied. So, what we think we want changes constantly, and we spend our whole life looking for something to make us happy.

> *The obstacle(s) to getting that which God wants for us arise from telling God our plans and putting our attention in the world of illusion where Truth can never be found.*

A Course in Miracles reminds me: "*It is, perhaps, not easy to perceive that self-initiated plans are but defenses with the purpose all of them were made to realize. They are the means by which a frightened mind would undertake its own protection, at the cost of truth.*" **W-pI.135.14:1-2** All God wants for us is the happiness and peace that comes through experiencing the fullness and joy of our Divine nature, which is our salvation. The obstacle(s) to getting that which God wants for us arise from telling God our plans and putting our attention in the world of illusion where Truth can never be found.

On the other hand, if you want to be guided from within to take a particular form of action, as I was to write this book, not because it is important but because it is simply a part of my process, then you need to be *willing* to *listen* and to act *only* on that guidance. Let that be the equivalent of you helping yourself. Spirit will be doing all the work for you and making sure that all that you need for the completion of your assignment is provided. All you need to do is *be still, listen* and let your inner guidance take you where you need to be. In a nutshell, *trust* in spite of circumstances. Or I should say, in spite of *illusions*.

The key is to set all your self-initiated plans (goals) aside and put God (peace) *first*! Let God take the reins so you can *enjoy* the ride of your life! Doing something contrary to the norm, like letting God lead while you just go along for the ride can come across as scary, when in reality it is just *different*.

Things Happen In Divine Timing

When people write their goals, set up deadlines, visualize what they want, etc., and then surprisingly their expectations don't come to fruition, the concept of "universal timing" is given as an excuse. Well, just for the record, universal timing does actually exist; it just doesn't work the way most people would think. It occurs when you have an idea, or inspiration, and feel *naturally* moved to take some sort of action. That is *when you flow with life* as opposed to when *you try to control it.* It was only when the time was right for me to move to California, write my books, and produce my music CD that it happened. So, you can also think of universal timing as the *true* definition of what is often referred to as "the right time."

Nouk Sanchez and Tomas Vieira, authors of *Take Me To Truth Undoing The Ego*, put it this way:

> *"As we develop that core of peace within, we realize that true creativity and insight are born from this expanded Self and not derived from the limited mechanical process of thought. True inspiration always comes from beyond the finite, leading us toward liberation."*

When I spent all my time visualizing, affirming, and trying to make things happen my way, I was constantly faced with opposition, discomfort, and pain. Every door seemed to close on me, and during those times, when I did get what I thought I wanted, I paid a huge price. So, if goal setting and visualizing what you want is not working, the ego will use the idea of "divine timing" as a tool to keep you *hoping*. This is another powerful tactic by the ego to ensure that you keep your attention grounded on illusions and away from Truth. This kind of attention keeps your hopes up for getting some kind of temporary pleasure or pseudo happiness. Remember that hope is the carrot at the end of the stick that will keep you going from seminar to seminar, guru to guru, teacher to teacher until you stop looking for the answers outside and start going within. Then you'll come to realize that *everything* you have always wanted and spent your whole life hoping for was at the *other* end of the stick. *The end you have always being holding.*

You Must Know What You Want

A Course in Miracles reminds me: "*Your function here* **is only to decide against deciding** *what you want, in* **recognition** *that* **you do not know.** *How then can you decide what you should do?* **Leave all decisions** *to the One Who speaks for God, and for your function as He knows it.*" **T-14.IV.5:2-4**

This one is the core of every self-help program on the market. False idols have all sorts of tools to help you get what you want, but you must first know what that is. But what if you don't know what you want? For that, all sorts books, seminars, teachings devices (more illusions) were developed in order to help you find what that is. Once you have found what that is, or I should say, you *think* you have found what that is, then, the coaches are there to make sure you follow through. It is a no-win situation.

I would like to share with you a quote, which I think you'll appreciate. It is by licensed practitioner, Ron D. Blair, who once said: "*When you let go of what you think you want, what you really want reveals itself to you.*" Think about this for a moment. What is it that you think you want? Most people would say, that which will bring them happiness. And what could this be? More money, a romantic relationship, more friends, a new car, a new house, more sex, toys to play with, the freedom to do what they want? According to *A Course in Miracles*, these are the little things this world has to offer.

> *When you let go of what you think you want, what you really want reveals itself to you.*

So in order for you to open yourself up so that what you really want reveals itself to you, or to be more specific, *through* you, you *must* learn to be okay with not knowing what you want. You may think you know what you want but that is *impossible* because what you *truly* want, at a much deeper level is to *remember Who you really are*. The things of this world of illusion simply keep us wanting one thing after another, leaving us *never* satisfied, *always* chasing. They are nothing more than *ego's distractions*. Some may say that they love the chase, but what happens before and after the chase? What choices do they have when they are not chasing something? Boredom, depression, unhappiness, distress, uneasiness, there is one word to describe that type of living. It's called *hell*!

Does that mean that there is anything wrong with going after things that bring excitement and joy to us? Absolutely not! I enjoy the process of writing this book. And when I am not working on it, I am perfectly fine with just being. No goals, no pressure, no agendas. *Just being*. Interestingly enough, the more I am being, resources needed to finish whatever project or task I am inspired to do naturally manifest, not because anything I do is important, but because that has been my experience. So by me not knowing what I want, you could say that I do know what I want. Whatever that is reveals itself to me in divine *timing*.

What Is In It For Me

One thing I noticed when I attended many seminars, and I am talking not only business but also so called "spiritual seminars," many people's seeming openness was not based on genuinely wanting to know one another but in seeing what they can get from one another. And that is because many teachers believe that their source and supply really comes from other people. That's why they need to manipulate their attendees through persuasive means. There is certainly nothing wrong with offering a service and being compensated for it. I get compensated when I speak and when I sell books and so on. The difference is that I don't see the *need* to manipulate anyone into purchasing what I have to offer. That does not mean that I will not advertise, unless I am guided not to. I simply *trust* that whoever needs to hear what I have to say will be led to me, not because I have anything important to say, but because there must be something for me to learn.

Returning back to the subject at hand, the only way I would be concerned about "what is in it for me," is because if I believe in separation, I begin to see giving and receiving as two completely different things, as an exchange. However, in oneness the giving and the receiving are one and the same, because when you are giving, who are you giving to? Yourself! Therefore in the giving *is* the receiving. *A Course in Miracles* reminds me: *"To give a thing requires first you have it in your possession. Here the laws of Heaven and the world agree. But here they also separate. The world believes that to possess a thing, it must be kept. Salvation teaches otherwise.* **To give is how to recognize you have received.***"* W-pI.159.1:2-7

Perception Makes Projection

The assumption here is that what you perceive is what you project. So if something is happening to you, which you don't like or is not supportive or makes you feel pain, etc., then by changing the way you see it or I should say "perceive" it, you can feel better, solve a seeming problem, change it or whatever the case may be. Somebody once said, *"When you change the way you look at things, the things you look at change."* There is some truth in changing the way you see things and I'll elaborate further within this section.

The challenge with the "perception makes projection" statement is that in order for you to perceive anything differently, you must *first* have to project it. That's why *A Course in Miracles* reminds us that projection is what makes perception and not the other way around. Many Teachers don't understand this concept because they are not aware of a simple detail. And that is, the original projection is what could be referred to as original sin, original error, the world of illusion made up by the ego. Remember that because the ego separates, compartmentalizes, analyzes, perceives just so that we continue believing that we are separate from God, no matter how many times you try to perceive things differently out in the world, that which you are trying to

> *...no matter how many times you try to perceive things differently out in the world, that which you are trying to perceive differently comes from a projection that is erroneous in the first place.*

perceive differently comes from a projection that is *erroneous in the first place.*

The projection is erroneous because it is *not real.* By trying to perceive differently, all we are doing is trying to rearrange hell in order to transform it into Heaven. And that is *impossible* because we are *already* in Heaven; all we need to do is stop *giving power* to the illusion of hell. In other words, instead of looking at hell and trying to fix it, waking up from the illusion will make it disappear. The only way out is by letting the One Who can interpret *righteously* to interpret for you. *A Course in Miracles* reminds me: *"Do not make the mistake of believing that you understand what you perceive, for its meaning is lost to you. Yet the Holy Spirit has saved its meaning for you, and if you will let Him interpret it, He will restore to you what you have thrown away."* **T-11.VIII.2:3-4**

A Course in Miracles also reminds me: *"Perception seems to teach you what you see. Yet it but witnesses to what you were taught. It is the outward picture of a wish; an image you wanted to be true."* So it could be argued that if you wish for something to look different, you can change your perception. However, that which you wish to change came from that which *you were taught*, a wish based on separation; the original sin or error; the ego's projection. And to change it for anything other than Truth is to exchange one illusion for another. As a result, our permanent peace is replaced by the *never-ending cycle* between pain and pleasure.

A Course in Miracles reminds me: **"The Holy Spirit can hold your magnitude,** *clean of all littleness, clearly and in perfect safety in your mind, untouched by every little gift the world of littleness would offer you. But **for this, you cannot side against Him** in what He Wills for you."* The line I want you to pay close attention to is: ***"But for this, you cannot side against Him in what He wills for you."*** **T-15.III.6:1-2** It is the understanding that you must decide which side you are on, God or your ego? In other words, peace or your problems, and I mean *all* your problems (the world that we seem to live in). Only the One Who can see the Truth can perceive correctly. We cannot do that because whatever we perceive at the level of the intellect will *always* be perceived through the ego's perception of reality.

Nothing Has A Meaning Unless You Give It A Meaning

We have to be careful with that because any meaning we give to an illusion will only lead to solidifying one's belief in the illusion. Many teachers use the changing of a meaning approach as a tool for what they would consider as personal empowerment. Although it may seem that way from an illusory standpoint, it will not lead to awakening to the Truth. Just about every other self-empowerment tool, the premise for these teachings is based on the belief that the body is real and what we feel is true. So when utilizing the changing of meaning approach they figure, *"if our thoughts create our feelings, and how we feel is based on the meaning we give to our experiences, by changing the meaning of any particular experience, we change our thoughts about the experience resulting in pleasant feelings."*

It may seem like a very effective form of therapy but the results are just temporary. From that perspective, the real problem will not be solved by changing its meaning; it will merely be covered by layers of meanings. That being the case, are we really solving the issue? No, all we are doing is piling up more and more guilt in the unconscious mind therefore adding more blocks to the awareness of love's presence.

To this you may say, *"Even if it is not solving the issue, as long as I feel better that's fine with me."* Although, I can understand where you may be coming from, there is a very critical point that is missing. The ego's purpose is to make you feel awful, miserable, and separate from God. Remember that real freedom lies not in giving meaning to any part of the illusion, but in understanding that *nothing* has any meaning at all. The reason you don't want to give anything a meaning is because it is *not* important. And the reason it is not important is because *it is not real!*

Since true answers cannot be found within the realm of the intellect, we can't rely on anything we tell ourselves. We simply have to rely on the One Who knows the answers. And these answers come in a form of experiences that lead us to oneness, as opposed to just a good feeling or feelings of pleasure. Because remember, in order to feel good, you must first have to feel bad. So your whole life becomes a tug of war between feeling good then bad, then good again for what you will have to spend your *whole life* analyzing (**anal**-yzing) your way through it by giving a meaning to this and to that.

A Course in Miracles reminds me: *"Sin shifts from pain to pleasure, and again to pain. For either witness is the same, and carries but one message: 'You are here, within this body, and you can be hurt. You can have pleasure, too, but only at the cost of pain.' These witnesses are joined by many more. Each one seems different because it has a different name, and so it seems to answer to a different sound. Except for this, the witnesses of sin are all alike. Call pleasure pain, and it will hurt. Call pain a pleasure, and the pain behind the pleasure will be felt no more. Sin's witnesses but shift from name to name as one steps forward and another one back."* **T-27.VI.2:1-9**

When most teachers say that nothing has a meaning in and of itself except the meaning that you give it, *A Course in Miracles* would say that nothing has a meaning in and of itself, *period*! The moment we attempt to give something a meaning, even if it could be considered a "pleasant" or "right" one, all we are doing is opening up a brand new can of worms. Remember, we are already inside a can of worms. It's called the physical world; the world of illusion, the world of separation; the realm of the ego. So to even try to give meaning to anything is like getting deeper inside the can.

Yet, it is so much simpler to just say, *"I don't know."* And be okay with that. Just let go and simply *trust*. The only way out of this mess is by allowing the Holy Spirit to take care of all meanings; for He is the One Who can lead us out of our self-made nightmare. A minister's answer to one of his students many years ago was, *"Remember that there are always two sides to any story.* ***And then there is the Truth."***

So instead of trying to give meaning to anything, just be. And the appropriate meaning will reveal itself to you in due time if *necessary*. This time, however, it will be a *righteous* meaning, one that will lead to liberation as opposed to further imprisonment. In a later chapter, I'll share how easy the process of letting our seeming challenge be interpreted by the Holy Spirit really is.

People Know What To Do But Don't Do What They Know

I was having a conversation with a friend, and she had invested a lot of money in "how to become rich" programs, just like I have in the past. Although these programs are sitting on her shelf collecting dust, I asked her why these programs were not working for her. Not wanting to admit the fact that she wasted all her money on these programs, she simply said that they do work; it is just that she is not applying what they teach. From a logical standpoint (ego), that makes perfect sense, and to an extent, there could be some truth to that depending on a variety of factors which we don't really need to get into because they are not relevant to our discussion. But if you dig a little deeper, you realize that there is a reason for not doing what you know. And that is because it is very difficult to do what you know when that which you know is not in alignment *with your path*.

Speaking strictly in dualistic terms, only for this chapter, if someone loves real estate, for example, and he is willing to spend hours on end on the computer doing research, searching for properties, studying the market, etc., he can put a weekend program together with tapes and books and sell them to you for a significant amount of money. The question is, are you as *passionate* about real estate as he is? If you are not, why did you purchase the program in the first place? Two reasons: One, because you were *not* sold on the *process* of making money in real estate, you were sold on the *idea* that you can make a lot of money and second, your emotions being the ego's magical weapon used against you, is what the teacher *manipulated* in order to persuade you to buy the program. Number one rule in marketing is, people make decisions based on emotions and then *justify* them with logic. Since the ego is always trying to justify itself it will come up with logical reasons, or you could say intellectual defense mechanisms in order to justify anything. The ego can come up with logical reasons as to why you should hate someone, even when that goes against your natural state of being, which is pure love.

So, if I can keep you in a state of fear or excitement, I can easily make you buy stuff you would not even need. Basically, your *lack of trust* in *your Self* makes you a *perfect* target for anyone to manipulate you. I often suggest to people to *never* make any decisions when they are in a state of fear or excitement, *especially* when they are in a state of excitement or being pressured. Simply practice being still *before* making *any* decisions. From a peaceful state of mind you are more apt to listen to your inner guidance, which in turn, will lead you to attend a particular seminar, *if necessary*, or to invest in something that is more congruent with your personal path.

Motivation

This is a very popular term employed by many teachers. People spend hundreds and thousands of dollars on coaches and teachers to help them stay motivated. But have you noticed that motivation seldom works? Why is that? Just like visualization, it is *not* natural. Most people need motivation in order to do something they don't want to do. If you don't want to do something, why do it then? If you know *Who you really are*, and make peace your number one priority, your motivation is replaced by *inspiration*. A Course in Miracles reminds me, *"Inspiration is of the Holy Spirit, and certainty is of God according to His laws. Both, therefore, come from the same Source, since inspiration comes from the Voice for God and certainty comes from the laws of, God."* **T-7.IV.1:2-3**

When you let go of all your agendas and stop trying to force things to happen, that's when inspiration strikes. *A Course in* Miracles reminds me: *"There is but one interpretation of motivation that makes sense. And because it is the Holy Spirit's judgment* **it requires no effort on your part.***"* **T-12.I.3:1-2**

> *When you let go of all your agendas and stop trying to force things to happen, that's when inspiration strikes.*

The truth is that you *don't* need motivation to do anything. All that you need is to *cultivate* a *peaceful* mind and to *practice trust*. Remember, however, that this book is not about teaching you how to get what you want, for that is *nothing* compared to what God Wills for you. *A Course in Miracles* reminds me: *"O my child, if you knew what God Wills for you, your joy would be complete!"* **T-11.III.3:1** It is about helping you wake up from the dream, where you believe you are separate from God, to the realization that you are in a state of Oneness where any seeming lack or limitation *cannot* exist.

The Why Is More Important Than The How

This one goes hand in hand with motivation, because the key is to develop a strong reason as to why you want something in order to have the will to move towards it. Where most teachers miss the point is in *thinking* that the "why" is something *you* need to *manufacture*. The truth is the why is *already* built in *within* the inspiring thought that emerged through you, as opposed to whatever self-made plans you may try to come up with.

The biggest mistake I see in the self-help arena is that all these self-proclaimed experts study people who have accomplished great things and through questions they try to lay out a road map for others to follow. They would be asking them why they felt so inspired to do what they did. Although the one being questioned may come up with all kinds of answers, at the core, the answer is the same. And that is, "I don't know, I just felt inspired to do it." Ask Picasso why he loved to paint. Ask Michelangelo why he loved sculpting.

Do you get my point? Let's take it one step further. Why is it that most of these self-help gurus and "experts" *love* to do research and to share passionately what they have discovered, *even when they do not seem to be able to apply the principles they teach to others to their own lives?* Is it because maybe what they *love* to do is to *teach*?

So if you ask anyone who is *passionately driven* to do what they do, or for the sake of this example, to do all the research and analyzing and trying to come up with answers, just so that they can teach it to others, if they are willing to put their ego's aside, *even if it means putting their reputation at risk*, they would have one answer, which would be, *"I don't know, I just feel inspired to."*

Why am I writing this book you may ask? For the same reasons I have produced my music CD, and did everything I have done with my life. Because I felt *inspired* to, and instead of *questioning* my desires, I just *went for them*. Right now I could come up with all kinds of logical reasons as to why I am writing this book. Yet at the core I know why. And that is because *I have to*. Not as a goal with a particular deadline, but for reasons not known to me. And I am pretty sure that after I finish this book, I will be led as to what to do next. *It is that simple*. All I have to do, is to let go and *let God*!

Do What Others Have Done And Experience The Same Results

Adding to what I just shared in the previous topic, another promise of the teachers of the "how to" seminars, is that if you do what others have done, you can experience the same results. English poet Edward Young once said: *"Were are all born original. Why is it so many of us die copies."* The voice of inspiration that I invite you to listen to is the same voice *that Jesus, Buddha, Mohamed, Gandhi, Dr. Martin Luther King Jr., Mother Teresa* and every saint and sage that have walked and still walk among us listens to.

Just for clarification purposes, if I want to start a business, for example, there is nothing wrong with consulting someone who knows about it in order to assist me in the process. Here is the key, when I am in a place of trust and surrender, I am presented with the *right* opportunity that will lead to where I am supposed to be.

Whatever results you need to experience that are in alignment with your personal path *will take care of themselves*, once you do what you are guided to do as opposed to what you *think* you need to do. I quote often these words from Jesus: *"Behold the fowls of the air: for they sow not, neither do they reap, nor gather into barns; yet your heavenly Father feedeth them. Are ye not much better than they?"* **Matthew [6:26]**

> *...how can you experience your uniqueness when your whole life is spent trying to be like someone else?*

Besides, how can you experience your *uniqueness* when your whole life is spent trying to be like someone else? I warn you however, it is very easy to do what others are doing. It is very easy to fit in. Trusting yourself seems discomforting and fearful at times. That will require *courage* and *strength*, for in listening to your True Self, most of your decisions may be in *direct opposition* to the world at large.

I don't know who is going to publish this book or how everything that needs to be done after I finish this manuscript will fall into place. All I know is that as of this moment all I can do is write what is coming through and that's all. As I am sitting in this beautiful library in Southern California looking out the window watching the ducks swimming in the pond, and the beautiful park and trees, it occurs to me that I may go for a walk later and just be in the moment. If I feel inspired to write more I'll do so.

I would also like to add something to this section. There is a very popular concept used by teachers in order to label people who begin projects and not always finish them. It is called *"self-sabotage."* Here is the challenge. Remember when I said that people know what to do but don't do what they know because it is very *difficult* to do what they know when that which they know is *not* in alignment with their personal path? Gosh, that was a long sentence wasn't it? Anyway, that's one true reason why most people can't follow through. Not because they are lazy, not because they are irresponsible, not because they are not passionate, not because they are "sabotaging" themselves, but because *they are forcing themselves* trying to go against their natural flow of their path. So the "self-sabotage" concept is just another guilt tool employed by some well-meaning teachers to get people to do what *they* want them to, or they think their students, clients, or followers "should."

What if in the larger scheme of things they were led to start something and leave it half completed just so that maybe in one, three, five, or ten years later they can finish it? That's what happens to me over and over again as I let go and trust. A song I wrote ten years ago is now touching the lives of many. A tape I produced in the mid-nineties is now opening doors for me to speak, where before all doors seemed to be closing on me as I kept forcing things to happen. So if you want to experience your uniqueness, then start listening to your *Self*. If you rather pay others to show you how to be small, they'll be happy to teach you how to think like *someone else,* which soon you will discover that it is *impossible*.

> *...the "self-sabotage" concept is just another guilt tool employed by teachers to get people to do what they want them to, or they think they should.*

To be, do, have, or to do, have, be, what was the question?

In most communities it is being taught that in order to be happy for example, one needs to *do* something first in order to *have* something so that he/she can *be* happy. So people find themselves *doing* whatever it takes in order to *have* whatever it is they think they need in order to experience, or *be* whatever it is they want to be. Which for the sake of this example would be, the experience of happiness.

Then a new teaching was introduced, which is a reversal of what was commonly taught, and that is, that in order for us to experience let's say happiness, we need to *be* happy first. Then as a result of our state of *being*, we find ourselves *doing* things that are congruent with our state of being (happiness), resulting in *having* whatever it is we want.

So if I want to experience abundance for example. I first have to *be* in that state. As a result of being in that state, I then find myself *doing* something that reflects that state of being. Finally, from doing whatever it is I am guided to do I will experience or *have* abundance. For some it could be having lots of money, for others it could be lots of friends, opportunities, support, etc.

> *The only thing to BE is PEACEFUL. Seek that experience always, and you are less likely to be deceived by the ego's game of separation.*

So whether you choose the "do, have, be" or the "be, do, have" the challenge is that both of them have the same agenda, which is, to seek an experience in this world that is already a part of you. Love is not something that you seek by being, doing, having or by doing, having, being. It is your *natural inheritance*. But as long as you find yourself seeking the experience in whichever form you choose to, all you are doing is adding to the belief that what you are seeking you don't already have, therefore *adding more blocks* to the awareness of love's presence.

The only thing to **be** is *peaceful*. Seek that experience *always*, and you are less likely to be deceived by the ego's game of separation. And from that space of peacefulness, you are more likely to have all these experiences you were once longing for, if in some way they truly serve you. You'll be led as to what to do, if it's necessary, and life unfolds from there as you continue to withdraw your attachment from anything this world has to offer. In other words, *choose God first*, and all these things will be added on to you.

Choosing peace through non-attachment allows for you to be led back home by the Holy Spirit, which is the *ultimate* experience. In the meantime, you can have a great time while being a part of this dream, except that you are not disturbed by it. *A Course in Miracles* reminds me, *"There is a way of living in the world that is not here, although it seems to be. You do not change appearance, though you smile more frequently. Your forehead is serene; your eyes are quiet.*

And the ones who walk the world as you do recognize their own. Yet those who have not yet perceived the way will recognize you also, and believe that you are like them, as you were before." W-pI.155.1:1-5 And that, I have to say, is one lesson I had a hard time learning.

Your Beliefs Determine Your Destiny

From the ego's point of view, you can say that the statement is accurate, because whatever you believe to be true is what you'll see. What you need to be aware of is that whatever it is that you are seeing is not True, it is just a belief, therefore leading you further away from the Truth; from experiencing *Who you really are*. A Course in Miracles reminds me: *"What keeps the world in chains but your beliefs? And what can save the world except your Self?"* **W-pI.132.1:1-2** Dr. Wayne W. Dyer, someone who has never been afraid to challenge the status quo once said that the difference between a belief and a knowing, is that beliefs are handed to you while a knowing comes from within. Therefore as a result of holding on to your beliefs, you are bound to experience more and more suffering. *A Course in Miracles* also reminds me: *"Where truth has entered errors disappear. They merely vanish, leaving not a trace by which to be remembered. They are gone because, **without belief**, they have no life."* **W-pI.107.1:3-5**

The world being an illusion, all you are seeing is a projection of what you believe to be true for you because it is seen through the lenses of the ego. An example would be that you are experiencing financial challenges. You then go to someone who can assist you in changing whatever unconscious belief or as some may say, limiting patterns you think you have, that are not letting you experience abundance. Here is the danger. *Who you really are* is *already* perfect, whole and complete, needing *nothing* and lacking *nothing*. However, because of your false sense of identity, you have made up a *belief* that you don't have enough, which is what the world represent given the fact that our experience here is one of separation. So changing that belief for another is not helping you access your True Self, one that is already abundant, infinite, perfect and whole. All you are doing is *exchanging* one belief for another, in other words, one illusion for another. So the ego is the one still running your life, you just feel a bit better, temporarily I may add, because you are experiencing your idea of "abundance." What's wrong with that you may ask?

That the ego's mantra as I already mentioned is *seek and never find*. What that means is, as long as you *believe* you are this false sense of self, although you may project some interesting illusions, they all come with their opposite as well. So you may project the illusion of having the person of your dreams and right before your eyes the relationship turns into your biggest nightmare. Or you may project the illusion of having the money you want just to discover that a few months later you end up with a terminal illness. Or you are afraid now of losing it. You may experience the fame and fortune you so much strived for and the demands of your new wish makes you more prone to depression or suicide because nothing this world has to offer will bring you permanent happiness, joy nor fulfillment.

That's why it is said; *"Be careful what you pray for because you may end up getting it."* I want to remind you once again that there is nothing wrong with having amazing experiences. But as long as you side with the ego, you'll *never* experience *permanent* joy and happiness because you *think* that your source of happiness, peace and joy is found in this world that not only you have made up but that it is *not even real*.

The following illustration will give you an idea of what happens when you let ideas, beliefs and opinions clutter your True vision; God's vision.

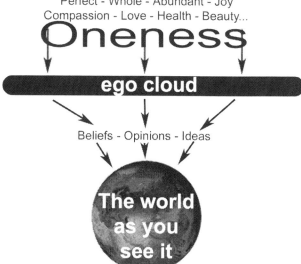

A Course in Miracles reminds me: *"When you made visible what is not true, what is true becomes invisible to you."* **T-12.VIII.3:1** For you to see that which is True, which cannot be seen with the body's eyes, you simply need to let go of what you see and think is true. Therefore, the key that holds your freedom has to do *not* with exchanging one belief for another, but in *letting go* of *every single belief* you have and be *willing* to admit the fact that *you don't know*. Only then can you allow yourself to be guided out of this illusion you have made up for yourself. A Course in Miracles reminds me: *"The Holy Spirit will always guide you truly, because your joy is His. This is His Will for everyone because He speaks for the Kingdom of God, which is joy. Following Him is therefore the easiest thing in the world, and the only thing that is easy, because it is not of the world."* **T-7.XI.1:1-3**

My question to you is, are you willing to let go of everything you think you know? Every opinion and belief you think is true? Are you willing to let go of all the titles that qualify you as an "expert?" Are you willing to let go of all that education and the diplomas you have acquired that reinforces your belief in thinking that you know best or that who you are is whatever title you think you've earned?" *A Course in Miracles* reminds me: *"The giving up of judgment, the obvious prerequisite for hearing God's voice, is usually a fairly slow process, not because it is difficult but **because it is apt to be perceived as personally insulting.**"* **M-9.2:4**

> *Following Him is therefore the easiest thing in the world, and the only thing that is easy, because it is not of the world.*

Instead of spending your time and energy trying to figure things out and/or exchanging one belief for another or figuring out your hierarchy of values and try to match them with your goals, etc., letting go is like becoming like a little child who knows that she doesn't know, therefore is not afraid to ask. That's why *A Course in Miracles* reminds me: *"The Bible tells you to become as little children. Little children recognize that they do not understand what they perceive, and so they ask what it means."* T-11.VIII.2:1-2 *"Verily I say unto you, Except ye be converted, and become as little children, ye shall not enter into the kingdom of heaven."* [Matthew 18:3]. The difference now is that instead of asking another guru or teacher, in other words, another false idol for answers, this time you are asking the One that can offer you Truth as your answer, the Holy Spirit, the part of you Who remembers *Who you really are*. And if there is a particular teacher or mentor you are supposed to see, let the Holy Spirit guide you to it, give the fact that that mentor is in your mind, only projected outward.

If You Do What's Hard, Life Becomes Easy

This belief implies that if you sacrifice yourself and do the hard work up front, then everything else after that becomes easy. Keep in mind that the sacrifice and hard work up front is nothing but the work you *think* you need to do in order to achieve an illusory goal that you *believe* will bring you happiness. However, regardless of whether you achieve what you thought would bring you comfort or not, you are *still* being deceived by the world of illusion, the realm of the ego.

Another point I want to share is, if you make up a monster so to speak, after lots of hard work and sheer determination, now you have to *maintain* it, which indeed could become your *greatest prison.* In that sense, what would be the point of sacrificing in order to go after anything, while in the process of working so hard you end up stressing yourself out or developing high blood pressure, a stroke, or some other kind of physical, mental or emotional imbalance?

From personal experience, what I have discovered is, not that if you do what's hard life becomes easy, but that if you *flow* with life, then life becomes easy. And how do you flow with life? You do so by resisting *nothing*, by practicing *non-attachment*. And that requires *trust*, letting go of control. For years I struggled so hard to make things happen and they either eluded me, or when I got what I wanted, I either ended up losing it, a whole new set of problems surfaced or it did not bring me the permanent joy or satisfaction I was expecting from it. Now that I am doing what I am called to do, I am just amazed as to how my life is unfolding *easily* and *effortlessly* as I continue to write the words you are reading.

> *...what I have discovered is, not that if you do what's hard life becomes easy, but that if you flow with life, then life becomes easy.*

Although from an outside perspective you may say that as of this moment financially I don't have it all together, from the inside, I am experiencing peace, at least in this moment, while I am able to continue to write this book *without* the distractions of what most people think I should be doing. Not only so, The Course helped me understand why life unfolds the way it does, which I'll elaborate on in a later chapter.

Before continuing, I would like to point out that the purpose of this chapter is to simply compare two different thought systems, Spirit's VS the ego's. So even when some of your beliefs might have been triggered, as The Course will *definitely* do, all I ask of you is be patient. Believe you me, that when I had to let go of *everything* I thought I knew, especially after writing four books, producing inspirational CDs and DVDs, having spoken at venues and coached others worldwide, it wasn't a very pleasant experience. Now that I have let go of all that I thought I knew, after experiencing the peace, the joy, and the creativity that springs forth as a result of just being, I wish I would have let go a long time ago.

Human Beings Do What They Do Because Of The Need To Avoid Pain And The Desire To Seek Pleasure

This misconception right here is at the core of all of our problems. The world being an illusion, just as our human body is, for it is part of the ego's projection in order to make us believe that we are separate, the ego then uses the body and emotions as its *number one weapon* to keep us away from experiencing our True Self. Can you think of anything more frightening to you than the anticipation of pain? Whether it is physical, emotional or psychological pain, our fear of pain would drive us to move towards anything that would make us feel better. That seems to make perfect sense except that we forgot that the body does not feel any pain. Only a mind filled with fear and guilt; a mind that thinks it is a body, projects unto the body what is experienced as pain.

To this, the logical reasoning would be then to change our mind in order to not feel any pain. The answer would be yes and no for reasons that will become clear to you as you read further chapters. For now, without deviating from this topic, since the body is an illusion and the world we live in is not real; being a projection of the ego as was already mentioned, the body is nothing but what gives the ego a sense of identity. Because we experience our sense of separation mainly through our physical body; our physical senses, emotions such as pain and pleasure can dictate what we believe is true for us. So if I feel pain, it seems real. If I feel pleasure, it seems real. *A Course in Miracles* reminds me: *"Pain demonstrates the body must be real. It is a loud, obscuring voice whose shrieks would silence what the Holy Spirit says, and keep His words from your awareness. Pain compels attention, drawing it away from Him and focusing upon itself. Its purpose is the same as pleasure,* **for they both are means to make the body real.***"* T-27.VI.1:1-4

This is the distraction that keeps us away from our Truth. It keeps us distracted, looking for the answers where they will *never* be found, within the intellectual realm or out into the world; a world that we are *projecting,* for as within so without. Since most believe that the body is real and that our emotions dictate what's true or not, there are teachers who needed to come up with answers to make sense of what they *think* drives human (ego) behavior, which according to them is our emotions, and how to *hopefully* being able to control them. And even when many teachers think they have found the answers, they are still baffled by the fact that most of their students can't put the principles they are being taught into practice. And by now you get a sense of why that is. But wait until you see the *real* reason, which will be discussed in a later chapter.

Since our True Self has no needs, but the body seems to think that it does, illusions were projected in order to justify the ego's behavior. Some of those illusions were labeled as needs while others, although mislabeled as needs, simply arose from the deepest core of our being. *A Course in Miracles* reminds me: *"A sense of separation from God is the **only** lack you really need correct. This sense of separation would never have arisen if you had not distorted your perception of truth, and had thus perceived yourself as lacking. The idea of order of needs arose because, having made this fundamental error, you had already fragmented yourself into levels with different needs."* **T-1.VI.2:1-3** Following are some of those ego needs.

The illusion of needing significance

According to the dictionary, significance is the quality of being worthy of attention; importance. If you know *Who you really are*, one with God, one with everything, perfect love, not of this world, what kind of significance would you possibly need? Only an ego who thinks it is separate and less important would need to scream out loud, *"look at me, I need attention, I need to feel important..."* Someone grounded in his/her True self, *detached* from false identities, does *not* need any kind of significance. Abraham Maslow once said: "*The highest quality that a human being can reach is to be **independent** of the good opinion of others.*"

The paradox however, is that those who do not need any kind of attention or significance end up getting the most. Someone who is *being* loving receives the most love. Someone who is *being* attentive receives the most attention. Someone who is *needy* needs to manipulate and persuade others in order to get something that he/she thinks is missing in his/her life.

The illusion of needing certainty

Certainty of what? That things will go my way? The truth is, at a human level you can be certain of one thing and one thing only. *That you have no control over anything.* You can make yourself believe that you do, but in reality you don't. You can go for what you want whole-heartedly and you may get it, but you can be certain of one thing, sooner or later you'll get bored with it and you will have to come up with ways to entertain yourself. Not to mention that you may lose what you get, or that now you have to protect what you think you have or that complications may result from what you worked so hard for. And that is because that's how the ego operates. Or, you can strive, fight, go after whole-heartedly for what you want, and still *never* get it! That's what I called the *hard way* of discovering the *Truth*.

But what if you let go and *trust* that *everything* is happening in divine order and that you need *not hang on to anything*? If you choose to do that, you'll experience *peace*. And you'll realize that the *only* certainty that you need is the knowing that *everything is being taken care of.* "But if all is being handled and I am at peace" you may ask, "*does that mean that I cannot have fun? That I cannot do things that require physically demanding activities or that I cannot focus on winning in a competitive sport or savoring the experience of accomplishing anything?*"

Although I am not here to reinforce the illusion of the body, I am going to answer that question at the level that it is being asked. If you stop focusing on winning, and simply stay *in the moment*, your performance is more likely to lead you to winning the game. Even then, you still have no certainty that you will win. However, after you have done your best, regardless of the outcome, you can walk away, be at peace and be appreciative for the opportunity to play in the game. But if you are attached to an outcome, by not being present, you will spend the whole time stressing yourself out before the game, and then feeling miserable after if you don't experience the desired outcome.

For example, even when I am very engaged in writing this book, I am at peace knowing that it is unfolding as it will. And I am pretty sure that once I finish it I will feel wonderful. But even as I am writing it, I am *not* attached to finishing it, although it seems that's the way I am heading. I feel no pressure, I have no deadlines, having the *certainty* that everything is unfolding as it will. Or I can simply suffer by resisting what is. And yes, you can have as much fun as you want. As a matter of fact, that is one of greatest things The Course reminds me of, to *not take life so seriously. A Course in Miracles* reminds me: *"Into eternity, where all is one, there crept a tiny, mad idea, at which the Son of God remembered not to laugh."* **T-27.VIII.6:2** And the reason for not taking anything seriously is because none of it is real.

The illusion of needing uncertainty

When you let go and let God, uncertainty has no power over you because deep within, you know that you are taken care of, and that everything is unfolding *perfectly*. You may feel a bit excited about the adventure, not because you need it, but because it *naturally* brings out the joy in you. The need for uncertainty is just a story the ego made up to make you believe that if you are uncertain, that brings excitement to this illusion. I don't know about you but I am excited peaceful for just being.

The illusion of needing love/connection

This one is an oxymoron because it is not a need; it is simply a *natural expression of your being* when you allow your True Self to come forth. You being One with God, and God being One with everything, love is *Who you really are* and to share it with everything and everyone is just what you do. And the connection you have with others is simply the connection you have with *yourself*, because we are all One!

The illusion of needing to grow

As I explained in an earlier chapter, I would say that the need is not to grow but to *remember*. To remember what? To remember *Who you really are*. So if growing to you means having more stuff, or chasing more goals, or acquiring more power, knowledge or attention, you are not really growing, you are simply *deepening your sleep*. But if growing means to deepen the connection with your True Self, that is not a human need, that is what you'll have to experience sooner rather than later when you come to the realization that this world of illusion cannot offer you anything of value, which leads to nothing but suffering.

The illusion of needing to contribute

Just like the previous two, this is not a need; this is part of your True Nature. If you are One with God, and all that God loves to do is to extend *unconditionally*, that is just what you do when you realize *Who you really are*. The challenge is, the ego contributes, or I should say, gives to get. In other words, the need for contribution comes from a place of needing attention or aggrandizement, or power. True giving, from the highest place, *does not* need *anything* in return.

Now you may ask, *"But how can you give without getting anything in return?"* Because when you remember *Who you really are*, someone that lacks *nothing*, you are simply contributing from your *inexhaustible* well of wealth, which has nothing to do with material goods, its really love. Secondly, when you know that we are all One, who are you really giving to? *Yourself*! That's what is meant by *"in the giving is the receiving."* This is something that intellectually cannot be understood for it won't make any sense.

> *But how can you give without getting anything in return? Because when you remember Who you really are, someone that lacks nothing, you are simply contributing from your inexhaustible well of wealth.*

Knowing now that you have no needs, nothing is lacking in your life and that pain and pleasure cannot have control over you once you start to awaken, you realize that truth can only be found *not* within the realm of pain and pleasure (physical body) but within the realm of peace (Heaven). The reason being is because peace is the conduit through which we can listen to the voice of the Holy Spirit or Higher Self. So really the pain that we are trying to get away from and/or the pleasure we are going after as well as all these seeming needs and wants, are nothing but the ego's manipulative ways to distract us from our peace. And that is because if we allow peace to enter into our awareness, the life of the ego is put in jeopardy. So the ego uses pain and pleasure as tools to ensure its survival.

After what I have said so far, running away from pain, at least for the purpose of awakening *is not always the best choice* and here is why. *A Course in Miracles* reminds me: *"...This ultimately reawakens spiritual vision, simultaneously weakening the investment in physical sight. The alternating investment in the two levels of perception is usually experienced as conflict, which can become very acute. But the outcome is as certain as God."* **T-2.III.3:8-10** As we begin to awaken, the transition between what we believed to be real up to this point, which is our physical world of illusion to what *Reality* is, our *True* nature, that seeming conflict can be experienced as painful and/or discomforting. So moving away from that pain is not going to help us awaken from the illusion. That's when we must be willing to allow the Holy Spirit to guide us through this *seeming* discomforting process, which I'll elaborate on more specifically in subsequent chapters. And by the way, if you find yourself in a situation where you may be in physical danger, I am not suggesting for you to be foolish and pretend you are invincible by not paying attention to your natural response to flee. Although you could say that in reality, as Spirit, you are invincible, at your current level of awareness (yourself as a physical body) that is not your experience. So you remove yourself from that situation altogether if you can, and then you bring yourself back to peace, which is not something you can do on your own for reasons that will become clear later.

For now, understand that no matter what we are running away from or moving towards, at the level of the ego, that is going to lead us to more pain, and/or suffering. It is a never-ending rollercoaster that we will *never* be able to get off of unless we choose to experience *Who We Truly Are*. **And that will only take place when we prioritize peace above all.** In letting go, that is *exactly* all we are doing. And the advantage of having peace is that for once we are able to listen to that still voice within that is trying to lead us to *Truth*.

There are teachers who I have seen go as far as to say that peace equates death. *A Course in Miracles* reminds me*:* *"There is a risk of thinking death is peace, because the world equates the body with the Self which God created. Yet a thing can never be its opposite. And death is the opposite of peace because it is the opposite of life.*

And life is peace." T-27.VII.10:2-5 They are so engrossed in the world of the ego that all they try to teach is how to manipulate our human emotions as a way to experience success and happiness and fulfillment, not realizing the *disservice* they are doing to their students. And that is because true happiness, joy, fulfillment and every single quality of our God's Self *cannot* be experienced from the things of this world. We can experience them while in this world, but not by means of the ego, only through listening to that still voice within that says; *"Be still and know that I am God."* I like to share an excerpt from an article written by Reverend Hugh Prather titled *Infatuation* regarding our emotions:

> *"The ego part of us loves to obsess on our emotions.*
> *For example, many interviews with winners of game shows, athletic competitions, pageants, award shows, and political contests begin with the question, 'How are you feeling right now?' --as if one's emotions were the most important consideration.*
> *Even in therapy, emotions are often the central subject of discussion and changing the client's prevailing emotion the central goal.*
> **To our ego, our emotions are our deepest self.**
> *Within our spiritual core, peace is the all-inclusive emotion, because it is one with God, one with Truth.*
> *A Course in Miracles points out that to be in the Kingdom is to focus your full attention on it. It therefore follows that* **to be at peace is to be your Self."**

As I am bringing this chapter to and end, another thing I would like you to be aware of, is that after twenty years of following and even teaching self-empowering techniques, getting to meet some of these well-known speakers, even working for one of them, I noticed a concurrent theme. Not for all of them, but for most, all that they want is money for the *false sense of power* they derive from it. Without it, they feel small. Not because they are, but because they *believe* they are, even when they are in denial of it. As a result, they even make others feel guilty for not having money. And they must, for that is how they can *manipulate,* or as they say, *"persuade"* others into investing in whatever it is they have to offer, *especially* when most believe, that you, me and everyone out there is their source and supply.

Unless people are dealing with a physical challenge in the form of an illness, which is the *only* thing that would distract them from pursuing whatever it is they *think* they want, everyone who listens to most self-empowering gurus, all they want is money. We live in a society that is driven by it. Here is a disturbing email I received before this book was published by someone who simply came across my website. These are her *exact* words, *without* any editing;

> *Dear Nick, I just wanted to say that I am so pleased I found your site. I feel that this law of attraction fever, is two far away from the truth. I listened to (name undisclosed) tele-seminar last night on attracting wealth and **it left me cold**.*
> *The questions were all from people wanting money. Not enough emphasis is being put on internal peace and strength. It took me a long time to realize this and forty years of searching, but mainly plumbing the depths. I gave up almost everything I had, ran my businesses down to virtually nothing and basically jumped empty handed into a void.*
> *What I found astounded me. Peace, happiness and a totally new way of life. It mended not just my broken spirit, but all my relationships with family and my beautiful child who had become separate from me spiritually. I am now in a position to retain the beauty I have found in my new life, while attracting to me **exactly what I need**.*
> *I found it interesting from my new perspective, that when you have peace and strength, there is little else you want, and attracting your needs is **enjoyable, fun and effortless**. You are a wonderful inspiration, and I believe that the world really needs you, now more than ever. With love, Sue. W.*

Am I saying that there is anything wrong with having money? Absolutely not, as a matter of fact, *feel free to have as much as you want and enjoy it!* I do enjoy it when I have it. There is no reason to feel guilty about having lots of money. What I am saying is, **be careful whom you choose as your god.**

The truth is, not having money is *not* the problem. The *real* problem is a two-point never-ending loop. The first problem has to do with the way you feel about not having it, and second, the *mistake* of *believing* that the way you feel has to do with not having it. In other words, if I feel bad for not having money, that triggers guilt and fear. Now that I am feeling fearful and guilty, and thinking that not having money is the reason I feel the way I do, that puts me in a very *vulnerable* position because I have introduced a new god (money) into my life. That forces me to keep my attention out into the world as opposed to where my attention should *always* be, which is *within*, in other words, on *God*. Even many people in the spiritual community don't want to accept that they have bought into the ego's way of thinking. That's why you hear titles such as, "spiritual prosperity" or "the law of spiritual abundance" or some other variation of the same premise.

Before putting this subject to rest, I'm now going to touch on something that may startle you. If anything I have said so far hasn't, I'm pretty sure this one will. Using myself as an example, as I was talking to a dear friend, I had a challenge sharing with her my experience because every self-help book out there keeps telling me that I should be careful about the words I use. So, if for example, I say I am broke, that means that my unconscious will translate that into reality, therefore prolonging my experience. What I was

> *There is no reason to feel guilty about having lots of money. What I am saying is, be careful whom you choose as your god.*

not realizing is that the underlying feeling of *pretending* that I wasn't broke was far more *lethal* than just saying that I was broke and then not to make an issue out of it. Just by *not* having to *pretend* or *defend* my position gave me such a sense of release. It was like a very powerful spiritual awakening. So guess what? I AM BROKE! And I'm okay with it. In the meantime what am I going to do, you may ask? Well, for once, I'm writing a book. Not that the reason I am writing it is to make money, but it could be a vehicle for me to generate income amongst other things. For you, it may be something else.

Remember that this book is *not* about making false gods out of things of this world but about remembering *Who you really are* first and foremost.

Before moving to the next chapter, a few reminders. These teachers or for that matter, any teacher I may be referring to in this book, do not exist. They are all my projections and therefore there is no reason for me to judge what they do or say, for in doing so I am only *judging myself.* I am simply using symbols in the form of words and sentences to convey a message. Finally, I want to remind you once again, if I were to believe that who I am is my body, or my identity or that this world is real, I would believe and happily teach most of what is being taught today by many wonderful and loving teachers. If this being the case, who in his/her right mind would not want to move away from pain and seek pleasure? However, someone in his/her *Right* mind, who can see illusions for what they are, would not be disturbed by pain or influenced by pleasure for he/she has experienced *the peace that passes understanding.*

Unfortunately for many of us, in order to achieve that state of peace so that we can remember Who we really are, we have to experience **this thing called suffering.**

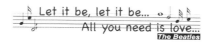

V
This Thing Called Suffering

"God did not leave His children comfortless, even though they chose to leave Him. The voice they put in their minds was not the Voice for His Will, for which the Holy Spirit speaks."
-A Course in Miracles [Text: chapter 5, section II, paragraph 6, sentence 8, 9]

"I will not leave you comfortless: I will come to you."
-Bible [John: chapter 14, verse 18]

You may wonder if there is a purpose for suffering or if suffering is necessary. When we experience our oneness with God, our True Self, there is no room for suffering. However, in our illusory physical form, where we mistakenly believe that who we are is this false sense of self, suffering is nothing but a guiding tool that forces us to let go so that we can experience *peace*.

By the way, let's not confuse suffering with pain. Pain could be experienced in many different forms. Physical pain, emotional pain, psychological pain; however, suffering is usually caused by *one* thing only. And that is *attachment*. It could be attachment to a thing, to a belief, to an opinion or idea, to an outcome, to a thought, or by resisting what is taking place in the moment, which is another form of attachment to how you think things should be. So you could be suffering *without* experiencing any specific form of pain or you could be experiencing an incredible amount of pain *without* suffering.

So what suffering does is bring us down to our knees. And there are two ways for us to get down on our knees. We either find that nothing in our lives is working no matter what we try, so we end up giving up, or we find that after achieving everything we thought we wanted, and still we do not experience happiness and fulfillment, we also give up. Even then, at least for most of us, before we finally turn our lives over to God, we try to look for answers from experts, gurus, or seminars, in other words, outside before turning within. That's why, although not always, the self-help movement can serve as a delay to our awakening. The reason being is because it will keep our attention out there, through entertainment and all sorts of ideas and illusions a little longer, *before* we are ready to really let go. *A Course in Miracles* reminds me: *"Everyone who follows the world's curriculum, and everyone here does follow it until he changes his mind, teaches solely to **convince himself that he is what he is not.**"* **M-in.4:4**

So what is the first thing we must do in order to release ourselves from suffering? We must let go of *all* resistance to what is. This may seem very difficult for most people, especially if they are faced with a seeming challenge. Here is an example, as I am typing these words, although my basic needs such as food and shelter have been met, the bank account shows around twenty dollars, the car I am driving has enough gas to get me back home, and I have no income coming in, at least that I know of, yet, here I am writing this book and being perfectly at peace. I am enjoying the beautiful view of this park as I type away what is coming through.

Why am I not suffering? Because I am *not resisting* what is and because I am *trusting* that I am guided and being taken care of. Right now, although getting a job may seem like a logical thing to do, in writing this book I am following my inner guidance *regardless* of what anyone may think or say. And I know that things will work out as they always have in the past, not according to any plan on my part, but according to the bigger plan. I am certainly not suggesting that you do the same, unless *you feel guided* to do so.

The second thing we must do in order to release ourselves from suffering is to *let go* of *attachments*. The reason people attach themselves to anything is because they think that that which they are attached to is either important or that they may lose something by letting it go. That's what takes place when people forget Who they are, yet their greatness is hidden under fear-based beliefs and ideas about who they *think* they are, how things should be and what they think they need or want. And to undo all those false beliefs, notions and ideas, they must be willing to *trust*, to *let go*.

> *The reason people attach themselves to anything is because they think that that which they are attached to is either important or that they may lose something by letting it go.*

I would like to share an analogy using the Niagara Falls as an example. Just imagine yourself being a part of a river that will end up at Niagara Falls. The flowing river represents your pure potentiality and the Niagara Falls is the *magnitude* of your greatness. If you *fight* the current, two things are happening *simultaneously*. One is that you end up *wasting energy* hanging on to everything you can, in other words, *suffering*. And two, you are *delaying* having the experience of discovering your magnitude. Interestingly enough, you *will* discover your magnitude because *it is your destiny*. Sooner or later you'll *have* to let go and you will end up at the Niagara Falls. *A Course in Miracles* reminds me: "*No one remains in hell, for no one can abandon his Creator nor affect His perfect, timeless and unchanging Love.* **You will find Heaven**. *Everything you seek but this will fall away. Yet not because it has taken from you. It will go because* **you do not want it**. *You will reach the goal you really want as certain as God created you in spinelessness.*" **W-pI.131.5:1-6** The question is however, how long do you want to prolong your suffering before you finally let go? How long do you want to continue trying to exercise control over your life and resisting what is, before you let go and plunge into the magnitude of your True Self? How long do you want to attach yourself to everything before you fully let go and trust?

Now, let's look at suffering from a different point of view by asking the following questions: *If I am made in the image of God, God being all that there is, why would God want me to experience suffering in order for me to wake up; to remember Who I Am? If God loves me so much why doesn't God wake me up?* The answer is simple, God is *not* having us go through the experience of suffering, *we are.* We are the ones who made up this whole illusion in the first place. We are the ones dreaming. And yes, through the aid of the Holy Spirit, we could say that God is trying to wake us up. But God is not interested in what we are dreaming about. God is just being. *God Is.* Not only so, God is *impervious* of what is taking place. We are the ones who chose to *believe* that we are separate from God by listening to the ego. God's arms are open, and ready to embrace us when we've decided to choose God over *everything* else. In other words, when we choose our Self, over illusions. And all we need to do is to let go. We don't even need to do anything else. No homework, no seminars, no how to do this or that, just *be* and allow the Holy Spirit to steer us in the direction of right-mindedness.

> *On this journey you have chosen me as your companion instead of the ego. Do not attempt to hold on to both, or you will try to go in different directions and will lose your way.*

A Course in Miracles reminds me: *"On this journey you have chosen me as your companion instead of the ego. Do not attempt to hold on to both, or you will try to go in different directions and will lose your way."* *T-8.V.5:8-9* So is suffering necessary for you to wake up, you may ask? The answer would be no. However, if you choose anything other than God (peace), *you are bound to suffer.*

So in reality, although we think we have many choices, we only have two, the choice to think with the Holy Spirit, or the choice to suffer by thinking with the ego. But we can't choose both, for it is *impossible* to be in heaven and hell at the same time, although, that's what seems to be happening. Instead of being in two places at once, we're in one place (home) having the *experience* of being in another.

So in reality, we only have one choice, for who would want to suffer? The obvious question now is, how can we wake up from this dream? Through *the power of forgiveness.*

> Let it be, let it be...
> All you need is love...
> — The Beatles

VI
The Power of Forgiveness

"The statement 'Father forgive them for they know not what they do' in no way evaluates what they do. It is an appeal to God to heal their minds."
-A Course in Miracles [Text: chapter 5, section V-A, paragraph 6, sentence 3, 4]

"Father, forgive them; for they know not what they do."
-Bible [Luke: chapter 23, verse 34]

In order to remember Who We Really Are, we need to let go of who we *think* we are. This false sense of self manufactured by the ego needs to be undone so that our True Self comes through. Our True Self is not something we need to search for, it is just *blocked* by layers and layers of ego. Yet in the stillness of the silence, it is whispering to us "*I Am*." In order for us to let the *I Am* shine forth, we must *first* forgive. Forgive who or what you may ask? Ourselves, or I should say yourself. Because, remember there is only One of you appearing as many.

This is how it works. Who we are is perfect, whole and complete. The world we see with our physical eyes and perceive through our physical senses is nothing but a *projection* of our ego. Even the body we are in is a projection of the ego, for it's the instrument through which we perceive *separation*. In *The Disappearance of The Universe* by Gary Renard it is summarized as follow:

> *"...you project your bodily image in the same way you project images when you're dreaming at night. Your mind is projecting a movie, then in your experience it appears that your body's eyes are seeing your own body as well as those other bodies – but it's actually your seemingly separated mind that's viewing its own thoughts, projected from a different, hidden level."*

Since the projection we see seems so real to us, instead of us observing it, we simply *react* to it. *A Course in Miracles* reminds me: "*The secret to salvation is but this:* **that you are doing this unto yourself.** *No matter what the form of the attack, this still is true. Whoever takes the role of enemy and of attacker, still is this the truth. Whatever seems to be the cause of any pain and suffering you feel, this is still true. For you would not react at all to figures in a dream you knew that you were dreaming. Let them be as hateful and as vicious as they may, they could have no effect on you* **unless you failed to recognize it is your dream.**" T-27.VIII.10:1-6

> **Since the projection we see seems so real to us, instead of us observing it, we simply react to it.**

So if I project the illusion of someone calling me a name for example, and I get angry, I simply reacted to something that is not real in the first place, something that *I* made up so that *my own* anger can be justified. That way I can have someone to blame for what I am not accepting or choose *not to see* in *me*. These are *the secret sins and hidden hates A Course in Miracles* refers to. The guilt that is deeply rooted in our unconscious, if not healed, we will continue to project it outward, therefore manufacturing the world that we see. Without a healed mind, we feel through our senses the seeming pain of what we claim is being done to us, therefore giving us reason to justify our blame.

Since God is oneness and the ego is duality, in the oneness of God all we can experience is love, happiness, peace, in essence Who we are. In the ego's world, on the other hand, all we see is separation, which leads to everything we experience in the physical realm. So when we see a world filled with anger, violence and hatred for example, what are we really seeing? *Our own* split mind projected outward, *our own* seeming duality looking right at us. So if we are all One and all we see is ourselves, when we are forgiving someone or something, as I said towards the beginning of this chapter, who is the *one* we are forgiving or what is it that we are forgiving? *Ourselves.* And here is the irony, what are we forgiving ourselves for? For having done *nothing*. *A Course in Miracles* reminds me: *"Forgiveness recognizes what you thought your brother did to you has not occurred. It does not pardon sins and make them real. It sees there was no sin. And in that view are **all your sins forgiven.**"* W-pII.1.1:1-2

The world sees forgiveness as something we are doing for others, as if we are forgiving them for something they have done to us. The Course sees it as a way to remind us of our innocence. And why would we want to forgive ourselves for everything we see happening in the illusionary world? Because, in order for us to experience the kingdom of God which is within, we must first clear all the blocks to the awareness of love's presence. Everything we react to that we perceive as real *must* be cleared before Truth can be revealed.

A word of caution, since the world that we see is made up by the ego, and forgiveness is the way to release the ego, you will encounter a lot of resistance from your ego-self. If you manage, for example, to forgive others for what they have not done, the ego then will try to use that guilt against you. The ego is then going to attempt to make you feel as if you are the guilty one for having projected the illusion. The message is the same for both. *None* are guilty. You are not guilty for the projection and the projection is not guilty for what it did not do. It's all a dream. It does not exist. *It's all made up!*

The next two illustrations will show the difference between the way the world forgives and how Jesus forgives. The following illustration shows how the world forgives, leaving us in a perpetual state of suffering.

As you can see, it is a never-ending cycle. And unless you are willing to forgive in a *true* sense, as shown in the following illustration, you will continue to experience the illusion of hell, even when you are actually safe and sound, only asleep in Heaven. The illustration below shows how Jesus forgives so that we can experience freedom from suffering and the realization of *Who we really are.*

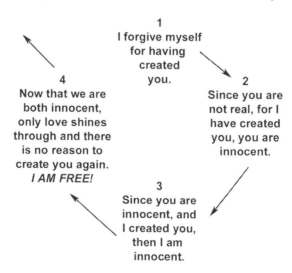

So the process of forgiveness is a circular process. We forgive ourselves for being the creator of the illusion. In forgiving ourselves for projecting the illusion, we acknowledge that the illusion is innocent. In acknowledging that the illusion is innocent, we are also acknowledging that we are innocent. In acknowledging that we are innocent, the hidden guilt that caused the projection in the first place is healed and therefore no longer needed to be projected. And if for any reason such an illusion should ever rise up in the field of our conscious awareness, our peace and happiness would not be disturbed. And thus we are free!

In *The Disappearance of The Universe*, author Gary Renard says:

> "...my attitude is that I look at the dream figures and I think, 'the guilt I thought was in you isn't in you; it's really in me, because there's really only one of us and you're just a figure I made up for my dream. I can forgive myself by forgiving you, and only by forgiving you, because you're symbolic of what's in my unconscious mind. If you're guilty then I'm guilty, but if you are innocent then I am innocent.'"

He then goes on to say:

> "It doesn't even matter if I appear to be forgiving the same images over and over again, because they may look the same, but it's really just more guilt that's being forgiven and released."

Through *True* forgiveness, as taught in The Course, we are able to experience more and more of our *unconditional* love. As more of that love reveals itself through us, we begin to see a different world. Or I should say, *the world the ego sees* begins to disappear and soon before we know it, we are ready to awaken from the dream.

The process of forgiveness applies to every single illusion you may find yourself projecting. That's why I added a second part to this book to address some of the most common illusions by themselves. So if you are open to what I have shared so far, then from a logical standpoint, the process of forgiveness will seem to make sense. Still the question remains as to how we can really put forgiveness into practice while feeling pain and discomfort from an illusion that, although we intellectually know it is not real, *seems* and *feels* very real to us? The answer is found in applying, **the process.**

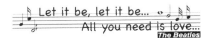

VII
The Process

"The knowledge that illuminates not only sets you free, but also shows you clearly that you are free."
-A Course in Miracles [Text: chapter 2, section I, paragraph 4, sentence 9]

"If ye continue in my word, then are ye my disciples indeed; And ye shall know the truth..."
-Bible [John: chapter 8, verse 31, 32]

As I shared before, from The Course and even from personal experience, in hindsight, I can see that the process does not need to be painful. However, the reason why it tends to be is because there are layers and layers of ego deep within our unconscious, that need to be undone *before* the light that is within us can shine through. When we let go and, in a sense what we are doing is giving up our false sense of self. That can be very scary, not because it intrinsically is, but mainly because the way we see ourselves, and the world, is all we know. And to give that up for something we don't know requires a great deal of *trust*, which is one thing that most of us are not always eager or ready to do.

Yet, if you knew that all you are doing is watching a movie that is not real, would anything that happens in this movie (physical world) matter to you or have any power over you? The answer is no. And yet, what makes it so difficult to just let go? The fact that you are more familiar with the ego than your True Self. You have identified yourself with your ego your whole life, while your True Nature, which is your natural state of being, is very foreign to you at your present level of conditioning.

Since all you know is your physical illusion through the eyes of your false self, the ego seems to be the one in charge. I said seems to, because in reality, God is the One in charge. Otherwise you would never be able to awaken from the dream. Presently, your belief in the ego is so strong that it is going to take some time to reverse it, so as you begin to awaken from your dream, the ego is going to do *whatever it takes* to stay alive. As a result, *especially* in the beginning, you are more likely to let your emotions dictate what is true for you. That's when the pain arises, because you have *conflicting* thought systems within you asking for your attention. The subtle difference is, the ego's thought system is *fighting* for your attention while the Holy Spirit's is *patiently* waiting *for you* to give it your attention, knowing that it is only a matter of time before you do. That's the choice you have, which reminds me of an old story about an old Cherokee Indian and his son. Here is how the story goes:

> *God is the One in charge. Otherwise you would never be able to awaken from the dream.*

> "One evening an old Cherokee told his grandson about a battle that goes on inside people. He said, 'My son, the battle is between two wolves inside us all. One is Evil. It is anger, envy, jealousy, sorrow, regret, greed, arrogance, self-pity, guilt, resentment, inferiority, lies, false pride, superiority, and ego. The other is Good. It is joy, peace, love, hope, serenity,

kindness, benevolence, empathy, generosity, truth, humility, compassion and faith.' The grandson thought about it for a minute and then asked his grandfather: 'Which wolf wins?' The old Cherokee simply replied, 'The one you feed.'"

So if you recall from the beginning of the book when I said that when you let go, two *complete opposite* thought systems collide, that can be a very disturbing experience. However, once you are open to letting go, you will be provided with the support you need in order to get you through some of your most discomforting experiences.

At this point you may ask; *"Why can't I just enjoy the world as it is and go for my goals and do what I want without having to go through all this waking up stuff, especially if it's going to be painful?"* First, it does not have to be painful, however, the answer to the question is, you can have the world you choose to experience. But the fact of the matter is, you'll soon have to wake up, because it is your True Nature. As I shared before, and worth repeating, *A Course in Miracles* reminds me: *"O my child, if you knew what God Wills for you, your joy would be complete! And what He Wills has happened, for it was always true."* **T-11.III.3:1-2** The world that you see, one with some seeming pleasures here and there, is doomed to bring you suffering. Yet, you have the choice to *accelerate* your awakening through forgiveness or to *delay it* through *suffering*, but not for long because remember that the ego wants to kill you. So your experiences here, not only will *not* always be pleasant, but your idea of yourself as being a body is going to end up in death. That's why the illusion of death came to be, as an attempt to give an end to something that is eternal. In the realm of God, in the Kingdom, which is *Who you really are*, eternal life is all that there is. Therefore death is not the opposite of life it is the opposite of birth. And the cycle of birth and death will stop, once you remember *Who you really are*. *"And God shall wipe away all tears from their eyes; and there shall be no more death, neither sorrow, nor crying, neither shall there be any more pain: for the former things are passed away."* **[Rv:21:4b]**

One of my favorite lines from The Course is when Jesus says; *"If you want to be like me, I will help you knowing that we are alike. If you want to be different, I will wait until you change your mind."* **T-8.IV.6:3-4** My understanding of that line is, truth will eventually have to surface regardless of how long you try to hide it or how much resistance you show before you are ready to recognize it. But recognize it you will, because it is a part of you. And the truth is simply this: *you are the Power and Presence of God!* You could also say that Jesus knowing what the consequences are when choosing a path laid out by the ego, He'll sit and wait until you run screaming back to Him asking for help.

And by the way, I've heard of well-meaning teachers who have quoted from *A Course in Miracles without understanding* what The Course is *really* about, suggesting that what Jesus is saying is that if I want to be like Jesus so that I can manifest whatever it is that I want in this world of illusion, He'll teach me knowing that we are alike. But if I want to be different, which by the way, given the choice of being like Him, I don't think anyone would want to be different, He'll wait until I change my mind. Yet again, if you understand the *actual* teachings of The Course, choosing a different way of looking at that same line, what Jesus is saying is, if you want to be like Jesus, meaning, *one with everything*, *non-dual*, **not of this world**, He'll teach you knowing that you and Him are alike. But if you want to be different, in other words, if you want to keep chasing the things this world of illusion has to offer, He'll wait until you change your mind. Which eventually you will because if you choose your illusions, sooner or later, you'll get hurt. This is the nature of this world. The ego gives and then takes it away, or gives one thing and takes another. But you'll *never* experience the *permanency* of your joy, peace, happiness and love, which is your *natural inheritance*, as long as you keep asking for the *blocks* to such awareness.

Another line from the Bible that sort of compares to the one in discussion, which is also heavily employed by most spiritual teachers is, *"Verily, verily, I say unto you, He that believeth in me, the works that I do shall he do also; and greater works than these shall he do; because I go unto my Father."* **[John 14:12]**. Lots of teachers love to *isolate* that line *without understanding* the place where Jesus is coming from. Prior to that Jesus says, *"The words that I speak unto you I speak **not of myself:** but the Father that dwelleth in me, **he doeth the works.**"* **[John 14:10]**. Notice that Jesus *never* talks about the work he does as having to do with his own individual will, goals or personal agendas, but that *everything* he does, such as the words he speaks and the works in the form of miracles, come from *His Father's Will*. One of the things I've always said since I started speaking at churches is that Jesus *did not* come here to manifest *anything*. He simply came here to *do God's work*. As a result of doing so, He could not help Himself but to experience miracles. Do you see the paradox?

With that out of the way, the awakening process is *very simple*, *not* necessarily easy, but simple. All it takes is your *willingness* to let go of the ego. And to do so, according to *A Course in Miracles*, is that there are six stages that we go through in order to undo the ego. The Course refers to them as the six stages of the development of trust. What these stages have done for me is allow me to understand what was taking place in my life as I went through them. As I am writing this book, I cannot say that I have achieved the six stages, but I have gotten glimpses of what I am capable of as I continue to undo the ego through letting go.

The actual process of awakening from the dream could differ from person to person. Gary Renard, author of *The Disappearance of The Universe* and *Your Immortal Reality,* was given a simple process to practice forgiveness and it goes like this:

> *"You are not really there. If I think you are guilty or the cause of the problem, and if I made you up, then the imagined guilt and fear must be in me. Since the separation from God never occurred, I forgive 'both' of us for what we haven't really done. Now there is only innocence and I join with the Holy Spirit in peace."*

I *strongly* suggest you get a copy of his books. Before elaborating on how I apply the process, and to show you how The Course is just one path out of many, I am going to briefly share about a healing modality from Hawaii called Ho'oponopono, which means to make right, just to demonstrate how it compares to the teachings of The Course *if* used *within* The Course's context. The reason I mentioned if used within The Course's context is because many traditions operate from the belief that the world is real. Although I am not suggesting that is what Ho'oponopono believes, that is the place where most healers and practitioners of different healing modalities appear to be coming from. They see the world of effects (illusions) and use their healing mantras or tools to attempt to fix what their eyes seem to see. The Course on the other hand, is *always* operating at the level of *cause*, from the level of *the mind*. It is *not* concerned with what we see because The Course *clearly states* that what we see with our physical eyes are *illusions*.

So without deviating from the teachings of The Course, let's see how Ho'oponopono could be employed as a tool for awakening. According to their practice, the words they use as their healing mantra are:

I love you
I'm sorry
Please forgive me
Thank you

If I use those words *within* the context of what The Course teaches, the *intention* behind them would yield the same results. For example;

Ho'oponopono: I love you
   ACIM: *I love you because you and I are one*
Ho'oponopono: I'm sorry
   ACIM: *I am sorry for having judged you*
Ho'oponopono: Please forgive me
   ACIM: *Please forgive me for having projected you or I forgive myself for having projected you*
Ho'oponopono: Thank you
   ACIM: *Thank you for letting me see what needs to be healed within me so that the Holy Spirit can correct it*

So how do I apply the process, you may ask? As *A Course in Miracles'* student, and also someone who loves simplicity, when confronted with someone or something that triggers fear, I release my concerns to the Holy Spirit for reinterpretation while *actively practicing* forgiving *everything* I see and *that's it!* At this point you may be saying; *"You mean just give it up to God and that's all? Come on Nick, there's got to be more to it."*

There is really not much to it, however I'll elaborate so you can understand what is really taking place. The body is an illusion projected by the ego and so is the world that we see. In order for us to make sense of what we see, we use the faculties of the intellect. So what do we do when we *try* to solve our deep unconscious guilt through the intellect, in other words, through the *illusion*? We are actually asking the illusion to get us to Truth. But that is *impossible*, because Truth is *beyond* the realm of the illusion, beyond the realm of the ego, in other words, *beyond intellectual understanding*. The ego *does not* know truth. All it knows is *separation*.

That being the case, Who is the only One Who can get you to Truth? The Holy Spirit. The problem is that the intellect wants a sequential, measurable, quantifiable order of specific instructions, presented in a manner that can be understood at the human level, before we can trust and let go. However, Spirit does not work that way. It simply needs your *willingness*, and *openness* to let Him dive in and start to undo the false sense of self you have made up. Nothing else on your part is needed. Remember, that although the process may be simple, it does not necessarily mean that it is easy. The following illustration shows why none of the intellectual approaches we try to apply to our human condition can work:

Iceberg Analogy

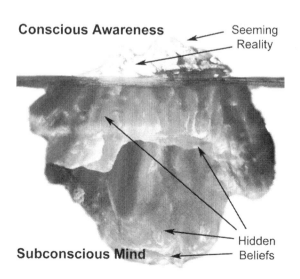

In modern psychology as well as with many spiritual counselors, the iceberg analogy is very popular because it is mostly based on changing beliefs. They say that what drives our behavior is what is taking place on a subconscious level. And since that is where our belief system resides, they try to use tools and techniques to try to change our beliefs so that we have a different experience on a physical level. However, there is a deeper part of our being that cannot be accessed through by anyone, and that is our ego. Only the Holy Spirit has access to it. Let's take a look at the following illustration before elaborating on why we can't access it.

Iceberg Analogy

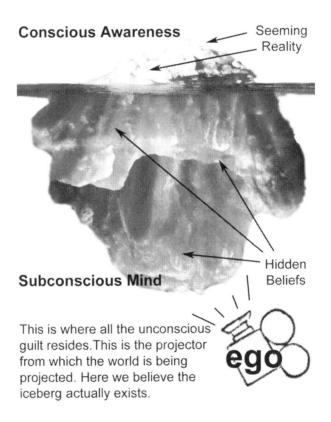

As you can see, the iceberg with all its beliefs, as well as our seeming conscious and unconscious mind, does *not* exist. It's all an

illusion being projected by this belief in our mind called the ego. Only the Holy Spirit has access to it, because it bypasses our conscious and subconscious human awareness. That's why I said before that changing one belief for another is just exchanging one illusion for another. Again, the reason why changing beliefs never solves our problems is because that which is in charge of the projector is the ego. And even when one belief may seem better than another, if we let the ego run the movie, suffering is inevitable. But if we let the Holy Spirit take over, *even when we are still experiencing ourselves as being part of the illusion*, the Holy Spirit first will teach us how to change our perception about our experience, and then through the collapsing of time will run the projector and *gently* start fast-forwarding the movie to the end, so that we can leave this movie theater filled with darkness and return to the light.

> *And why do you feel pain? Because of your lack of faith, your lack of trust is forcing you to hang on to something that is not real.*

So when you are willing to let go and let God, then the world, as you know it, begins to fall apart. How does that make you feel? The answer for most would be uncomfortable of course, and in many instances it is painful. And why do you feel pain? Because of your *lack* of *faith*, your *lack* of *trust* is forcing you to hang on to something that is not real. *A Course in Miracles* reminds me: *"When you try to bring truth to illusions, you are trying to make illusions real, and keep them by **justifying your belief in them**. But to give illusions to truth is to enable truth to teach that the illusions are unreal, and thus **enable you to escape from them.**"* T-17.I.5:4-5 As you *practice* it becomes easier to let go. You have practiced your whole life to believe that what you see is real and to be in control, and look how far it has gotten you. Now you are being given an opportunity to *practice* the *opposite*. So here is how *I* do the process:

1. When I am presented with something in my field of conscious awareness that triggers any kind of discomfort, I realize that I have been given an opportunity to practice forgiveness. I call this *the signal*.

2. At that moment, I simply say silently or out loud, depending on where I am, *"I do not know what anything, including this means. And so I do not know how to respond to it. And I will not allow my own past learning to be the light to guide me now."* **T-14.XI.6:7-9 Note:** You don't have to use the exact same words. Just having the right *intention* and the *willingness* to relinquish your thoughts, ideas and beliefs to the Holy Spirit *is all that matters*.

3. I make peace my *number one priority* while trusting that the Holy Spirit is doing the work. By the way, step 2 and 3 are interchangeable.

What is the purpose of this process? For me is to *disengage* the intellect. Some teachers use processes that require writing and intellectual searching. For some people that seems to work best. For me however, I like to keep things as simple as possible. I also stay away from anything that could lead to giving meaning to anything. That is a common ego strategy I have seen, especially with many students' responses to what they are learning in different courses. Something happens and they say, *"I guess that means that..."* The moment you find yourself uttering those words, you can rest assured that to some degree the ego (intellect) is involved.

That's why I said before, *A Course in Miracles* reminds me: *"Do not make the mistake of believing that you understand what you perceive, for its meaning is lost to you. Yet the Holy Spirit has saved its meaning for you, and **if you will let Him interpret it**, He will restore to you what you have thrown away."* **T-11.VIII.2:3-4** Remember that every time you say, "this means anything" you are deviating from Truth and *speculating* within the realm of illusion. If you can be okay with *not knowing*, you open yourself up to experiencing more peace as well as less or no conflict at all. That puts you one step closer to knowing the *Truth*.

Yes, the intellect does serve a purpose, however, not the one the ego wants to give it. Intellectually I know how to put these sentences together, turn this laptop on, use this program and do what bodies do throughout the day, in other words, *practical* matters. But that's about it. Anything else, all I know is that *I don't know*. As a matter of fact, my daily prayer is, *"God, please help remind me that when I think I know, that I don't."* To me, I found it to be such a *freeing* statement. For me, the less I know the more I get to *experience* freedom, happiness, and *peace* while finding it easier and easier to *trust*, to let go.

Does that mean that every time I practice the process the pain will be gone automatically? Not always. It all depends on how much resistance in letting go I may have. If there is a lot of ego to be undone, the discomfort may arise again, as it probably will, however, I allow the Holy Spirit to do the work until the guilt that once resided deep within my unconscious is being lifted. So I may have to apply the process multiple times. As I do however, I notice subtle changes letting me know that the process is working. The beauty of it all is, everything is done *bypassing* intellectual understanding. As I mentioned earlier, I *don't* need to do *anything*. That's why The Course says that spirituality is very simple but the ego is very complicated.

I would like to share one experience out of many on how the forgiveness process has worked for me. In the area of romantic relationships, a deep-seeded guilt would arise, and no matter how much therapy I sought, or who I talked to, or what books I read, or what written exercises I did, I could not get rid of it. As a result, I stayed single for almost twenty years. Then I met someone named Dawn. We cared a great deal for each other and became romantically involved. This time, the guilt feelings I had experienced in the past resurfaced, *stronger than ever.* I knew I cared about her, but wasn't sure about what I was really feeling. Yet, even though I was confused, torn apart, and in lots of pain, I still couldn't let her go. Then I felt resentful toward her, because unconsciously I would make her responsible for the way I was feeling. Now it gets even more interesting. I would feel guilty for not feeling sure if "she's the one," which of course, in a world of illusion there is no such thing as "the one", but at the same time I would feel jealous even of the thought of her leaving me and choosing someone else. That deep-seeded guilt within my unconscious *could not* be addressed intellectually because the ego was in charge of the projector from which the movie was being run.

As I started to practice my forgiveness process during those moments when I felt the guilt feelings arise, interestingly enough, those guilt feelings began to dissipate *naturally*. I noticed that in the past, that which would have triggered fear and guilt no longer had any effect on me. Let me tell you about a specific example where jealousy was the issue for me. One night when she was going to be attending a massage therapist convention, she wanted to save some money for hotels, so she suggested staying at her old boyfriend's house. For just a split second, I could see the ego wanting to intervene. Yet, I felt okay with that and did not make an issue about it. It just happened as a result of *applying* the process of forgiveness; by releasing *all* concerns to the One who can get to the root cause of all discomfort. So what is it that we need in order to apply the process and undo the ego? We need to start **letting go of control thru the development of trust.**

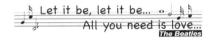

VIII
Letting Go of Control Thru
The Development of Trust

"'Many are called but few are chosen' should be, 'All are called but few choose to listen'. Therefore, they do not choose right. The 'chosen ones' are merely those who choose right sooner."
-A Course in Miracles [Text: chapter 3, section IV, paragraph 7, sentence 12 - 14]

"So the last shall be first, and the first last: for many be called, but few chosen."
-Bible [Matthew: chapter 20, verse 16]

Now that you understand the importance of forgiveness, to really put the process into practice you need to *trust*. Trust that there is a Holy Spirit doing the work, trust that there is such a thing as a Higher Self, trust that there is no world, trust in letting go and letting God, all while we are having a human experience that seems very real and that is constantly trying to convince us of the seeming reality of this world of illusion.

This is where you are asked to have faith, to make the decision to choose the Holy Spirit *always*, even if it seems scary, knowing that somewhere deep within, you are being prepared for your awakening. Still the ego will tempt you with promising goals and transitory experiences that you think are permanent and can bring you happiness. You will realize that *none* of the promises the ego makes are true. There is a line in The Course's Manual for Teachers that says: *"When he is ready to learn, the opportunities to teach will be provided."* When looking at that sentence, notice that the opportunities come in two ways; one in the form of illusions you are asked to forgive and two, in the form of support that will assist you as you move through this journey.

As you let go and let God, *A Course in Miracles* explains the six stages of the development of trust and undoing the ego. And these are;

1) The Period of Undoing
2) The Period of Sorting Out
3) The Period of Relinquishment
4) The Period of Settling Down
5) The Period of Unsettling
6) The Period of Achievement

Let's briefly elaborate on each, because this will become very helpful as you undertake this journey.

Stage 1: The Period of Undoing

During this stage, changes begin to take place in our lives in preparing us for letting go of what we value as important. *A Course in Miracles* reminds me: *"It seems as if things are being taken away, and it is rarely understood initially that their lack of value is merely being recognized."* **M-4.I.A.3:3** Since nothing of this world is valuable for it's all an illusion, when things we value most are being taken away, because we still haven't recognized the fact that they are meaningless, we seem to experience fear and discomfort. Not because of the experience itself, but because of our *lack of trust* in what is really taking place. The Course then says: *"How can lack of value be perceived unless the perceiver is in a position where he must see things in a different light?"*

In other words, while you are holding on to an illusion, you are not able to perceive the lack of value it has. But once it is taken away, and you finally let go, you are then in a position to see that which you thought was important in a different light. Meaning, from a place of *detachment*. Then you can really laugh at the silliness of your unnecessary suffering. This is not to be confused with the old saying: *"Time heals everything."* Time does *not* heal *anything*; it merely *hides* it until an opportunity comes up for it to be dealt with again. An example would be deciding that you need someone different after ending a dysfunctional relationship, (which you, of course, made up), and not realizing that you haven't healed the unconscious guilt that projected that relationship in the first place. In following this example, you will notice that when you bring that new person into your life, the old patterns *resurface*. Whereas when you practice your forgiveness process, you will notice that the purpose of time is for you to *truly* release that unconscious guilt that drives your behavior. So the time it takes to heal is relative to your unconscious attachments. Detach today and you heal today, detach tomorrow and you heal tomorrow, detach a thousand lifetimes from now and you heal a thousand lifetimes from now.

Stage 2: The Period of Sorting Out

At this point you have come to the realization that changes are taking place in your life. And even when you know intellectually that *all* changes are *helpful,* for they are leading you to your awakening, that does not mean that whatever it is you are presented with you will happily embrace or see it as helpful. And because there are still things you find important or valuable to you, you'll perceive the loss of them as sacrifice. *A Course in Miracles* reminds me: *"Because he has valued what is really valueless, he will not generalize the lesson for fear of loss and sacrifice."* **M-4.I.A.4:4**

The main lesson at this stage is to come to the understanding that *everything* that is taking place in your life, as scary or as painful as it may seem to let go, it's all part of your awakening process, it is *all* helpful. Most importantly, it shows where you still experience attachments, which is the *only* reason you experience pain and suffering. Just as with stage 1, you are given the opportunity to *discern* between the things and/or changes you still thought were valuable, except that with your increased awareness, you can now see how they were actually holding you back from your awakening. There is an old quote that says; *"You'll not be presented with something you cannot handle."* Therefore, some of the changes taking place in stage 2, although they were bound to happen sooner or later, unless you have done your forgiveness process more diligently, might have been a bit overwhelming for you to handle in stage 1.

And by the way, the changes that are taking place in your life are not just happening at random, everything is *perfectly orchestrated* by the Holy Spirit, so in reality there is no reason to fear; for you are *always* being provided for and taken care of. The more you learn to trust and let go, the faster you go through the stages.

If we were willing to follow and apply the teachings of Jesus, we would not have to experience the crucifixion. His whole message was that we have the power to experience the resurrection *right here and now*. The crucifixion we experience metaphorically, of course, is because we keep giving more attention to our ego than to the Holy Spirit. *A Course in Miracles* reminds me: *"Each day, each hour, each minute, even each second, you are deciding between the crucifixion and the resurrection; between the ego and the Holy Spirit. The ego is the choice for guilt; the Holy Spirit the choice of guiltlessness.* **The power of decision is all that is yours.***"* T-14.III.4:1-3 So what do we have so far? Nothing is valuable, every change is helpful and this second stage is giving us the opportunity to experience the helpfulness of each change through acceptance *and* as preparation for the next stage.

Stage 3: The Period of Relinquishment

At this stage, *A Course in Miracles* reminds me: *"If this is interpreted as giving up the desirable, it will engender enormous conflict."* M-4.I.A.5:2 The reason is, as we are being asked to relinquish everything that is valueless, and since *everything* in this world is valueless, all of the things we still have a desire for, in other words, have an *attachment* to, we are asked to let them go. And that could be a very challenging time, because as much as we may want to wake up from this journey, as much as we want to experience our True nature, we still hold onto things. We are asked to give up *all* attachment to things of this world, no matter how much we think we want or need them, so that the awareness of love's presence can be revealed through us.

The key to remember, especially during this stage, is that you *are not giving up anything* of value. You are simply letting go of the valueless so that you can experience your true greatness. Quoting once again, lesson 145 from *A Course in Miracles* reminds me: *"Beyond this world there is a world I want. It is impossible to see two worlds."* **W-pI.145.1-2** In other words, the world you truly want to see is *beyond* the one you can see with your physical eyes, with your ego-self. However, since you cannot see two worlds, the only way to see the one you *really* want is by relinquishing *all* that you see in this one as real. And the reason why it seems scary is because you cannot conceive of what the *Real* world is like.

At this point you have done a lot of work. Some people may have experienced physical or emotional challenges like depression, loss of personal things, career loss, relationship loss, amongst other difficulties that may have forced them to really see where they still have placed importance on what's not real. And that is because as the Holy Spirit removes the blocks to the awareness of love's presence, the ego is fighting for our attention. And all we can do is to continue *practicing* forgiveness while offering our thought system to the Holy Spirit. These are *very critical* times because when you think your life is falling apart, which in essence, it is, the truth is, you are actually going through an *inner transformation* where eyesight is being replaced by *true vision*.

Stage 4: The Period of Settling Down

A Course in Miracles reminds me: *"This is a quiet time, in which the teacher of God rests a while in reasonable peace."* **M-4.I.A.6:2** I call this stage "the treat." Because it gives us a chance to take a break from all the work that has been done. You may experience staggering success; things come into your life easily and effortlessly, you experience love *beyond* your wildest imagination, and a dramatic increase in peace. And even if your external circumstances may not have changed, just the fact that you are experiencing an enormous amount of peace allows you to see how much you have grown. However, the work is not done. *A Course in Miracles* says: *"He has not come as far as he thinks."*

The reason being, although we may have experienced amazing things, the thought system of the ego has not been fully undone. As a matter of fact, the ego wants to take credit for all these experiences. This stage can be very distracting. An example would be that after experiencing financial challenges your whole life, after doing the forgiveness work and realizing that nothing is of value, you find yourself having a sudden burst of financial success. At this point, you are enjoying life and getting caught up in the emotions and pleasures of your success, while forgetting that none of it is valuable. For a moment, you start losing sight of what the real purpose of this stage is.

In continuing to the next stage, *A Course in Miracles* reminds me: *"Yet when he is ready to go, he goes with mighty companions beside him. Now he rests a while, and gathers them before going on. He will not go from here alone."* **M-4.I.A.6:11-13** There is a reason why from this point forward The Course reminds us that ...*He will not go from here alone.* Most of what we thought we have worked through shows up in our lives once again, in order for us to see them from a higher perspective before they are finally released. For a better understanding, let's look at stage 5 next.

Stage 5: The Period of Unsettling

A Course in Miracles reminds me: *"Now must the teacher of God understand that he did not really know what was valuable and what was valueless. All that he really learned so far was that he did not want the valueless, and that he did want the valuable. Yet his own sorting out was meaningless in teaching him the difference."* **M-4.I.A.7:2-4** Using the example from the previous stage, the fact that you gave value to your new experiences, shows that you still don't know the difference between what is valuable and valueless. And even when the experiences might have been fun, they are valueless because they come from this world. They are *not real,* they are nothing but *illusions*, and because of their egoic nature, you are bound to experience suffering. You must always remember that the goal is *not* to exchange illusions within the dream but to wake up from the dream so that you can experience *Who you really are.*

Further on, *A Course in Miracles* reminds me: *"He thought he learned willingness, but now he sees that he does not know what the willingness is for. And now he must attain a state that may remain impossible to reach for a long, long time. He must learn to lay all judgments aside, and ask only what he really wants in every circumstance."* **M-4.I.A.7:6-8** Here is what is taking place. Willingness to let go is *not* about letting go so we can get what we *think* we want or experience anything in particular. We are simply willing to allow the Holy Spirit to do the work that it is instructed to do, which is to help us wake up from this dream. Our *willingness* to *trust* that whatever is taking place in our lives is happening as it should be, knowing that God is in charge and not us, in order for us to be in such a trusting and receptive space, we *must* first have to let go of *every single* judgment we have about *anything*. And even if we try to change anything by using our own will, at this stage our efforts become useless.

At this stage we could say that we have definitely let go of most of our guilt, however, there is still some guilt and attachments that we need to let go of. It is like a child who is willing to go wherever his mother asks without questioning, for as long as he is with her, he is safe and fully provided for. However, often times the child wants to make his own decisions, forgetting that the mother is still in charge. At that moment, the child cries, pushes, and pulls to get his own way, without being able to succeed; then the time comes when he will not only understand what took place, but, he will also appreciate his mother's decision.

So what happens at this stage is, as The Course reminds me; *...his own sorting out was meaningless in teaching him the difference,* we are presented with the things we thought we had already worked through, as I shared in the previous section, just so that we can reevaluate them from a higher place. This is when we are finally given the opportunity to see things *without* judgment, but instead seeing them for what they are, illusions that have no value. As we fully let go of any judgment and/or attachment to anything, the remaining blocks are finally released so that the awareness of love's presence can now be revealed through us. And in order for this to happen, we must do as The Course says: *"He must learn to lay all judgments aside, and ask only what he really wants in every circumstance."* And what is it that we really want in any circumstance? *Peace of mind* and *Real vision*.

That's all we need to ask for. From that space, *True* guidance is received, judgments are laid aside, attachments are released and an incredible sense of peace is experienced *even* within the illusion as we find ourselves becoming ready to awaken.

The Course says that attaining this new state of awareness *"may remain impossible for a long, long time."* It does *not* say that it *will* remain impossible, but that it *may*. The reason being is, we can *accelerate* the awakening process by our *willingness* to *practice* forgiveness. In that sense, it could be said that we could determine how long this stage is going to last. Borrowing the words from Tomas Vieira, co-author of *Take Me To Truth Undoing The Ego,* when a radio listener asked him how long does it take to undo this false self, his answer was, *"In hindsight I can say, as long as **you want** to continue to suffer."* To this you may ask, *but who in his/her right mind would want to continue suffering?* The answer is *nobody*. But as The Course reminds us, the process is simple, but *not* necessarily easy. If you *really* want to stop the suffering, all you need to do is to *let go of all attachments*. See how simple it is? Yet, why don't you? Let's leave it at that for now because pretty soon you'll see why.

Stage 6: The Period of Achievement

A Course in Miracles reminds me: *"This is the stage of real peace, for here is Heaven's state fully reflected. From here, the way to Heaven is open and easy. In fact, it is here. Who would 'go' anywhere, if peace of mind is already complete? And who would seek to change tranquility for something more desirable? What could be more desirable than this?"* **M-4.I.A.8:5-10** The emphasis here is not necessarily that the circumstances in the world that we see might have changed, but that our peace of mind *cannot* be disturbed. This is the *ultimate* place to be because from here we can experience what the condition of Heaven is like, we are now given the opportunity to experience the *permanency* of pure joy, love, peace, abundance, all that the Kingdom has to offer. *A Course in Miracles* reminds me once again: *"It is hard to understand what 'The Kingdom of Heaven is within you' really means. This is because it is not understandable to the ego, which interprets it as if something outside is inside, and this does not mean anything. The word 'within' is unnecessary. The*

*Kingdom of Heaven **is you**. What else but you did the Creator create, and what else but you is His Kingdom?"* **T-4.III.1:1-5**

From this space of non-resistance and non-attachment, free from judgments, filled with love and peace, although as I said earlier, our circumstances do not necessarily have to change, our new found peace, joy and happiness allow for the Holy Spirit to replace your nightmares with what *A Course in Miracles* refers to as the *Happy Dream*, which means that even when we have not fully awakened from this dream, we can still have an amazing experience before we do so.

The experience could range from being so happy and joyful *without* our circumstances having to change, to the experience of having the success and fun stuff we were once attached to given back to us; this time however, the fact that we are not attached to them allows for us to enjoy all of it even more.

The question often asked now is, *"During these seeming challenging times, especially as we go through these stages where fear seems to take over and our trust is being put to the test, how can we continue on?"* The answer is, through the powerful experience of ***the present moment.***

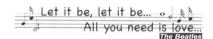

IX
The Present Moment

"Be very still and hear God's Voice in him, and let It tell you what his function is.
-A Course in Miracles [Text: chapter 29, section V, paragraph 5, sentence 2]

"Be still, and know that I am God."
-Bible [Psalms: Psalm 46, verse 10]

All our concerns, worries and fears arise from projections of a possible future or remembrance of past experiences. That worry is what blocks us from experiencing the peace we have available *only* in the present moment. I love the way Nouk Sanchez and Tomas Vieira talk about the present moment in their book, *Take Me To Truth Undoing The Ego*:

> "...we explained how our ego-self is preoccupied by either thoughts of the past or expectations of the future. It cannot exist in the here and now because, when we dissolve into the present moment, **we escape time and enter into eternity**."

Then they go on to say:

> The Truth here is that we, through our distorted thoughts and belief, projected whatever suffering we perceive exists in our reality today, either personally or collectively. To reverse this insanity we need to **learn to enter into the now moment awareness** because it is in this place where we gain a wonderful sense of sincere humility and Oneness. None of our past reference points remain **and we are literally free** from limitation; hence, no judging enters."

Even when the six stages of undoing the ego may seem a bit disconcerting, all they are doing is forcing us to enter the present moment. In that moment where ego cannot exist, we are open to the *direct* experience of communion with our Higher Self, free of suffering. Author Eckhart Tolle says in his book *A New Earth, Awakening to Your Life's Purpose*:

You can't argue with what is. Well, you can but if you do, you suffer.

"You can't argue with what is. Well, you can but if you do, you suffer. Through allowing, you become what you are: vast, spacious. You become whole. You are not a fragment anymore, which is how the ego perceives itself. Your true nature emerges, which is one with the nature of God."

Using myself as an example, as I am writing this chapter, there are lots of illusions taking place that could easily cause me to be concerned and to suffer, Iinterestingly enough, I have been mysteriously taken care of as I continue writing this book. Most importantly, *I am at peace.*

And how can I possibly be at peace when all of this seems to be happening around me? By *not* resisting what is. By being present in the now where there is no worry, no suffering and by also remembering that *none of it* is important, it is *valueless* remember? That does not mean I have to starve and do nothing. I am simply saying that I am trusting that everything that is taking place in my life is helpful and also being orchestrated *perfectly* in order for me to continue to develop *trust* and to practice *non-judgment*. All that is asked of me is to make peace my *most important priority*, to *listen* and to act on that *guidance*. Lesson 106 of *A Course in Miracles* reminds me*:* "**Hear and be silent**. *He would speak to you. He comes with miracles a thousand times as happy and as wonderful as those you ever dreamed or wished for in your dreams. His miracles are true. They will not fade when dreaming ends.* **They end the dream instead; and last forever**, *for they come from God to His dear Son,* **whose other name is you**." W-pI.106.4:2-9

As I sit in the stillness, regardless of illusions, and still feel that writing this book is what I am inspired to do, in spite of what logic may dictate, I'll continue to do so; because we must remember that in the realm of the ego, things may make sense, but that does *not* mean that they are true. It makes perfect sense to say that the sun rises every morning. However, what is really taking place, is that the earth rotates in order to give the illusion that the sun is the one rising. That optical illusion can be explained scientifically, however, the optical illusion you and I are a part of *cannot*, it can only be *experienced*. Liz Cronkhite, founder of *ACIMMentor.com,* has this to say about illusions and our experience.

> *"When you are struggling to grasp the concept of the world as an illusion, understand that you are trying to grasp this concept with ego, which will never grasp it. Let it go and don't struggle to understand it. You are just feeding the ego. Understanding will come with the experience of God. There is nothing you have to force on your way to God. You only have to be open to experiencing God and understanding will follow."*

Now that we understand the value of being present, let's move on to the next chapter by asking these questions; *If by being in the present moment I am guided as to what to do, why am I going through some of these experiences? And why is it that when I was given logical advice that seemed to work for others, I was not able to follow it? What was stopping me from doing what most people are doing in order to succeed or to get ahead?* And on a much broader scale, *why would I feel drawn to write a book while others are drawn to become scientists or doctors, secretaries, CEOs, missionaries, pilots, musicians, janitors and why are some born with seeming disadvantages while others seem to be born with a silver spoon? Is it karma? Is it luck? Is it evolution? What is it?* The answer lies in the understanding that ***the story has been told.***

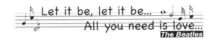

X
The Story Has Been Told

"I came to fulfill the law by reinterpreting it."
-A Course in Miracles [Text: chapter 1, section IV, paragraph 4, sentence 3]

"Think not that I am come to destroy the law, or the prophets: I am not come to destroy, but to fulfill."
-Bible [Matthew: chapter 5, verse 17]

This was one of the most challenging things for me to understand. I was like, *"What do you mean the story has been told? Don't I have free will? Can I not make things happen as I choose?"* A Course in Miracles reminds me: *"The world of time is the world of illusion. What happened long ago seems to be happening now. Choices made long since appear to be open; yet to be made. What has been learned and understood and long ago passed by is looked upon as a new thought, a fresh idea, a different approach.*

*Because your will is free you can accept what has already happened at any time you choose, and only then will you realize that **it was always there.**"* M-2.3:1-5

As I look at my life, I see the patterns that have taken place over and over again. And even after attending seminar after seminar and doing things differently, something deep within would not allow me to continue on with what I thought I needed to do. As I said in an earlier chapter, *I knew what to do but I could not get to do what I knew.* It was as if I was watching myself making decisions and could not do anything about making different ones. And just when I thought I was moving ahead, if it wasn't because I would get sick, all doors would simply close on me. If I applied for work, I would not get called. Work I had lined up, all of a sudden got cancelled. Just to give you a surreal experience that happened while I was putting together my online video class back in 2004, I had just finished a contract with a Cruise Line for about three weeks. I made around $7,500. On the cruise, I checked my emails everyday. When I got back from the trip, I saw an email sent by my agent asking me if I had the next six weeks open. When I replied to it, the contract was fulfilled. That would have been around $15,000. Here is the interesting thing, the email was sent to me *before* I did my previous contract and it showed up in my email box *after* I got back from it. Long story short, I found myself broke once again. Many things like that kept happening to me. It was as if no matter what I did, or how much effort I put in, it was useless.

So if this world is an illusion, all made up, and everything already has happened, then past and future do not really exist. However, if we seem to experience past and future, and the experience is not real, where is the experience taking place then? It is taking place *in our imagination*. We are making it all up! But if we are making it all up, can we make up what we want then? You could say yes, except that what we claim we are making up has already been made. And since what we are experiencing in this illusion is the duality made up by the ego, in order for us to experience our True Oneness, all we need to do is to awaken from this illusion.

So the purpose of forgiving is not so that we can experience a better life within the dream, but so that we can wake up from it. However, if we are having the experience of being here, through forgiveness we are given the opportunity to have a happier experience before we fully wake up. But how can that happier experience take place if the story has already been written? Because although the story has already been written, there are multiple possible scripts with multiple endings. In other words, each lifetime has its own script with its own beginning, middle and ending. However, through forgiveness we are given the opportunity to merge scripts, In other words, we are given the opportunity to *collapse* time so that we can have the ultimate experience we have been yearning for, the experience of *remembering Who we really are*. One last observation before sharing how this process works. Although we use the term lifetimes, which is another way of saying reincarnation, remember that there are no lifetimes and no reincarnation because the body *is not real*. All we are experiencing is different dreams. A child who is sleeping can have multiple dreams in the same night. So when we die, we don't awaken and then go back to sleep. Once you awaken, *that's it!* In the meantime, in between birth and death, you are experiencing a different dream until the guilt that is in your unconscious is healed.

> *...if we are having the experience of being here, through forgiveness we are given the opportunity to have a happier experience before we fully wake up.*

As human beings, since we experience life in linear time, our forgiveness process takes place in such a manner. We forgive memories from a seeming past that actually never happened. We forgive whatever illusion we are projecting in the moment, and we forgive thoughts of an imaginary future that has no basis in reality. However, in the realm of Spirit where time and space do not exist, every time we practice forgiveness, Spirit will work through every experience, every lifetime, going through past, present and future. So even when we practice forgiveness in the moment and we don't feel as if it is working, on a metaphysical level *it actually is*. And that's why we *need* to have *faith*. The following illustration gives you a visual of how this works:

Birth	Sept 15	Death
Lifetime 5	Watching television	
Lifetime 4	Camping with family	
Lifetime 3	Being at the hospital	
Lifetime 2	Dinner with friends	
Lifetime 1 → → → Without forgiveness	Being Robbed	Consequences

Using as an example five lifetimes out of many, which by the way, *A Course in Miracles* reminds me: *"The miracle substitutes for learning that might have taken thousands of years,"* **T-1.II.6:7** first notice that the illustration has a birth and death. That's not to be confused with Who you are because the Real You can *never* die.

So in the illustration, on September 15 you can see the different possible outcomes that could take place within each lifetime. Based on lifetime 1, if you do not practice forgiveness, you are bound to find yourself in a position where you may be robbed. After that event, there are consequences you'll have to deal with. Remember that this is something that *already happened*. However, if you practice forgiving yourself for having projected the illusions that are taking place in your life, the Holy Spirit uses that forgiveness to remove any guilt that caused those illusions, and for that matter, similar ones to appear in the illusory future while collapsing time. *A Course in Miracles* reminds me: *"The miracle shortens time by collapsing it, thus eliminating certain intervals within it."* **T-1.II.6:9** The following illustration shows what takes place when forgiveness is practiced:

Birth		**Sept 15**	**Death**
Lifetime 5		Watching television	
Lifetime 4	→	Camping with family	Consequences
Lifetime 3		Being at the hospital	
Lifetime 2		Dinner friends	
Lifetime 1		Being Robbed	
	Practicing forgiveness		

Holy Spirit Collapses Time

So because of your forgiveness process, having learned the lessons you needed to learn, time has being collapsed by the Holy Spirit. Now *on that same day*, not only you may find yourself having a different experience, but you are just one lifetime away from awakening, unless of course, you take advantage of your forgiveness process therefore making lifetime 4 your last. I would like for you to keep the following in mind: I chose the experience of going camping with family, *not* because it is better than any other one, but because in reality, as we awaken and release the guilt from our minds, we begin to see and experience the world *differently*. That's why *A Course in Miracles'* workbook reminds me: *"A miracle is correction. It does not create, nor really change at all. It merely looks on devastation, and reminds the mind that what it sees is false."*

We can be at peace, even in the midst of an accident. Because all we are going for is the *peace that passes understanding*. That is the peace we *must* acquire *before* experiencing the kingdom of Heaven. The peace, the joy that is congruent with our True Self, if we can be in that space *regardless* of our experience on earth, we have achieved *true* freedom. Once the guilt has been removed from our mind, there is no reason to have any further physical experiences.

No More Lifetimes!
No More Suffering!
Permanent Peace, Love Joy and Happiness!

Complete forgiveness

From this comes a very powerful realization. We were never afraid of our darkness, we were always afraid of our *light*. Our darkness is the world that we made up and we tenaciously hung onto it, for it was all we knew. Our light is the world we awaken to when we let go and let God. That's the *Real* world; the one that can't be seen with the physical eye or experienced with our physical body, but that *will* be experienced the moment we *awaken*. As we do our forgiveness process, we'll get glimpses of it, but to even try to comprehend it intellectually is *impossible*.

A Course in Miracles reminds me: *"Can you imagine what a state of mind without illusion is? How it would feel? Try to remember when there was a time, - perhaps a minute, maybe even less - when nothing came to interrupt your peace;* **when you were certain you were loved and safe.** *Then try to picture what it would be like to have that moment be extended to the end of time and to eternity. Then let the sense of quiet that you felt be multiplied a hundred times, and then be multiplied another hundred more.* **W-pI.107.2:3-5** *And now you have **a hint, not more than just the faintest intimation** of the state your mind will rest in when the truth has come."* **W-pI.107.3:1**

With that being said, all we need to remember is that God loves us *unconditionally*, and just because we find ourselves in this nightmare what we have made up, it does not mean that God has abandoned us. All God wants is for us to be happy no matter where we are or what we are doing. But for that to take place, we need to *trust* God's plan and *let go* of ours. At least for all I know, after twenty years of trying to do it my way, my plan has not being working. That's why from now to eternity I am choosing God's way by simply *letting go and let God!*

> **The hush of Heaven holds my heart today.**
>
> *Father, how still today! How quietly do all things fall in place! This is the day that has been chosen as the time in which I come to understand the lesson that there is no need that I do anything. In You is every choice already made. In You has every conflict been resolved. In You is everything I hope to find already given me. Your peace is mine. My heart is quiet, and my mind at rest. Your Love is Heaven, and Your Love is mine.* **W-pII.286.1:1-9**
>
> The stillness of today will give us hope that we have found the way, and traveled far along it to a wholly certain goal. Today we will not doubt the end which God Himself has promised us. We trust in Him, and in our Self, Who still is one with Him. **W-pII.286.2:1-3**

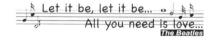

Part II
Application

Introduction Part II

"We thank You, Father, for Your guarantee of only happy outcomes in the end. Help us not interfere, and so delay the happy endings You have promised us for every problem that we can perceive; for every trial we think we still must meet."
-A Course in Miracles [Workbook: lesson 292, paragraph 2, sentence 1, 2]

"In that hour Jesus rejoiced in spirit, and said, I thank thee, O Father, Lord of heaven and earth, that thou hast hid these things from the wise and prudent, and hast revealed them unto babes: even so, Father; for so it seemed good in thy sight.."
-Bible [Luke: chapter 10, verse 21]

Although the Truth is simple as mentioned earlier, the ego is very complicated. And the intellect, which is run by the ego, wants to dissect and understand everything. The thing is, Truth *cannot* be understood intellectually. It has to be *experienced*. A Course in Miracles reminds me, *"Truth can only be experienced. It cannot be described and it cannot be explained."* **T-8.VI.9:8-9** Here in part II, I decided to share how I apply the forgiveness process to the most commonly troubled areas in most people's lives. And these are health, career, wealth and abundance, relationships, emotional issues, helping those in need and in forgiving specific individuals.

Before moving on, I would like to share, one last time, what is taking place in my illusion as I type these words, not that it is important, but why not share some illusory stories. The last few days have been very interesting; right now the two bank accounts are still in the negative, although a transfer deposit is on its way to bring them up-to-date; someone purchased a copy of my music CD with a check, the check bounced, so that diminished the balance and caused additional charges. Now, let's see what will happen between today and tomorrow, since the electronic transfer will not enter into my account until tomorrow and I presently have around 80 cents. Interestingly enough, I just finished a teleconference interview, which went amazingly well. These are just two of the comments I received:

> *Thanks Nick for telling me about the tele-seminar yesterday, it was great, because of you. You really did a wonderful job of simplifying the who, what, when, how, and where of connecting with our Source. You gave enough information so that a person can at least make that first step to being still to receive; when you stated that when feeling anxious to take a deep breath, ask for peace, and be still. -M. S., GA*

> *Hi Nick, I just finished listening to your interview. It was fabulous! You are really advancing in your work. You do sound really peaceful and grounded, and your message was very clear and confident,—it was a beautiful thing to hear. As always, all that you said rings true for me, which is encouraging and validating—let's me know I'm on the right track. I have to say I am so grateful to have met you. When I look back to where I was, and where my life was, a year ago when we first encountered each other, it is amazing to me how much I've grown. Thank you again for your loving guidance and encouragement. Your support and influence has really helped. Have a great evening, and Much Love to You. - J. L., CA*

In the midst of all this, I still have not found a place to work. Without causing you concern, I would also like to share what happened prior to that call today. As I was faced with all these apparent concerns, I had to leave the library. I got into my car and started to cry. It was getting to the point where I started to lose faith in God, and myself. Yet, while I was feeling those emotions, I was able to become the observer of what was taking place in my life. From that space, I felt more peaceful and remembered to forgive myself. I was not denying what I was feeling; I was simply honoring them while at the same time releasing them through forgiveness. Interestingly enough, today's lesson from *A Course in Miracles* is: "***I rest in God.***" A few sentences from that lesson; "*'I rest in God.' This thought will bring to you the rest and quiet, peace and stillness, and the safety and the happiness you seek. 'I rest in God.' This thought has the power to wake the sleeping truth in you, whose vision sees beyond appearances to that same truth in everyone and everything there is.*" W-pI.109.2:1-4

So I went on with my day, took a long walk around the park and decided to experience my abundance. And believe it or not, I felt very abundant *regardless* of the seeming situation. In that moment I was able to get a real sense of what true freedom is. To be able to feel abundant and peaceful and joyous *regardless* of circumstances, *this is the lesson to be learned from The Course.* Our peace and happiness are *not* dependent on our circumstances. One, because they are just illusions (not real) and two, because Who We Are (what is Real) cannot be defined by illusions, only Truth! As *A Course in Miracles* reminds me: "**Nothing real can be threatened. Nothing unreal exists. Herein lies the peace of God.**" ACIM Introduction

Now I would like to take the time to share how I apply the forgiveness process to whatever illusions I project in my world. Keep in mind that it is *not* about the words, it is about *your willingness* to do the process. Spirit couldn't care less about words so *do not* turn the forgiveness process into an intellectual issue.

♪ Let it be, let it be... ♪
All you need is love...
The Beatles

XI
Health & Healing

"All forms of sickness, even unto death, are physical expressions of the fear of awakening."
-A Course in Miracles [Text: chapter 8, section IX, paragraph 3, sentence 2]

"Heal the sick, cleanse the lepers, raise the dead, cast out devils: freely ye have received, freely give."
-Bible [Matthew: chapter 10, verse 8]

A *Course in Miracles* reminds me: *"The body cannot heal, because it cannot make itself sick.* **It needs no healing.** *Its health or sickness depends entirely on how the mind perceives it, and the purpose that the mind would use it for. It is obvious that a segment of the mind can see itself as separated from the Universal Purpose. When this occurs the body becomes its weapon, used against this Purpose, to demonstrate the fact that separation has occurred.*

The body thus becomes the instrument of illusion, acting accordingly; ***seeing what is not there, hearing what truth has never been said and behaving insanely****, being imprisoned by insanity."*

I had an interesting experience regarding healing of the body many years before I was introduced to *A Course in Miracles*. Keep in mind that when the course talks about healing is never about the body but about the mind. And what is healing, is the belief in separation. However, the mind that is filled with fear may project itself in what appears a body filled with sickness, in other words, fear being a cause, may produce an effect which is experienced as a sick body. On the other hand, and mind filled with peace, may also project itself as a body that would experience physical health. But once again, let's not make the mistake of thinking that the forgiveness process is to cure anything, it is always to reinstate the mind to its natural state of peace.

The way I handled it feels to me like at some deeper level I was being congruent with a few of the principles of The Course. Let me share a little bit about the experience. Around 2001, I started to feel sick and could not figure out what I had. The cause of the imbalance I would say was excessive stress and lack of career fulfillment. I went to a clinic close to home and although I had no clue what I was suffering from, one of the things I made clear to the physician was that I would not take any prescription drugs. I simply told him to figure out what I had so that I could find alternative therapies, if necessary. Well, it's a good thing I am strong-willed, because if I had allowed him to treat me he would have been ready to prescribe drugs. Not that there is anything wrong with prescription drugs, but just let me share what happened for me at the time.

After some blood tests and a few check-ups, a nodule on the thyroid was diagnosed. I was referred to an endocrinologist. After a few biopsies, a tumor was found. The doctor recommended having the thyroid removed. He even gave me the names and numbers of a few surgeons. I remember asking him; *"Are you familiar with the mind-body connection? Do you know who Dr. Andrew Weil is or Dr. Bernie Siegel is or Dr. Deepak Chopra is?"* And by the way, these are all medical doctors. With a nod of his head, his reply was no. On that day, something inside of me knew that I must stop seeing that doctor. That is *exactly* what I did. I never saw a doctor since and my health was *naturally* restored.

Yes, I know that what took place was an illusion. However, the point I am trying to make is about my attitude at the time I was experiencing the imbalance. My attitude was that if it was time for me to leave the earth, I would be okay with that, because I was not afraid of dying. Well, *A Course in Miracles* helped me understand what was taking place with the following sentences; *"The **only thing** that is required for a healing is a **lack of fear**. The **fearful** are not healed, and **cannot** heal. This does not mean the conflict must be gone forever from your mind to heal. For if it were, there was no need for healing then. But it does mean, **if only for an instant**, you love without attack. An instant is sufficient. Miracles wait not on time."*

Based on my understanding of the Course's teachings, the experience we are seeking is not a miracle in a form of physical cure, because the healing doesn't take place in the body, as I already mentioned, the healing occurs in the mind. This reminds me of the excerpt from the curse that states, *"The healing of effect without the cause can merely shift effects to other forms. And this is not release."* T-26.VII.14:2-3 What we are *always* seeking is the peace of mind.

Since my attitude was honest, that assisted me in experiencing a peaceful state of mind, which allowed for the healing to take place, *only* if that is what was supposed to happen. Because the ultimate goal in any situation is to be at peace, *no matter what* seems to be taking place in our illusion.

We *must* remember that the Holy Spirit does *not* judge like we do. Its judgments are based on truth, ours on fear. If my body had served its purpose and it was time for me to go, there was *nothing* any doctor or healing therapy would have been able to do to change the outcome of my destiny. The *only* choice to be made by me at the time, is the same one I have right here and now, and that is either to allow the Holy Spirit to bring me peace or allow the ego to worry me to death.

Now that you have read about my experience, understand that it doesn't mean that if you are moved to see a doctor and take their medicine, that you shouldn't do that. You must remember that the letting go of fear *must* be *genuine*; otherwise, all you are doing is *denying* your fear. So if you are fearful and believe that what the doctor has to offer would help bring you peace of mind, then go ahead and see the doctor. Because, remember, the Holy Spirit is guiding you to take whatever form of action is necessary to release some of your fear. That's why The Course says' "... *if only for an instant, you love without attack. An instant is sufficient.*" In that instant the Holy Spirit can do the necessary work.

I would like to share an excerpt from an article titled, *Misusing the Mind to Heal the Body* by Liz Cronkhite, founder of ACIMMentor.com. The excerpt reads:

> *"The ego uses physical illness and pain to make the body real to you. That is its primary goal for illness and pain. This shows up as using them for many reasons: To get attention, to punish you, to avoid situations, to make others guilty, etc. But of course no matter how physical symptoms show up their origin is in your mind. Ultimately all healing is the result of you accepting healing in your mind, either directly in your mind, or through "agents" like medicines, doctors, and treatments that seem outside of you and that remove the symptoms in a way that your mind can accept. Using external agents is what A Course in Miracles calls "magical thinking", but it is necessary until you can accept healing directly."*

Also *A Course in Miracles* reminds me*:* "*The body needs no healing. But the mind that thinks it is the body is sick indeed! And it is here that Christ sets forth the remedy."* **T-25.In.3:1–2** So how do you apply forgiveness when it comes to healing? Instead of identifying yourself with the body, you look at it for what it is, an illusion you are seeing being projected into the field of your awareness. You do *not* resist nor deny what you are experiencing, because by doing so you are at the *effect* of the experience. In other words, you are *reacting* to what appears. In reacting to what appears, all you are doing is making a judgment, which is the same as to say, you are making an interpretation. That in itself *solidifies* the illusion as being real. So *without* judging the illusion *or yourself,* you simply ask the Holy Spirit to bring you peace. Following that, you ask the Holy Spirit to reinterpret for you whatever it is you are experiencing, fully accepting the fact that *you don't know.*

Bringing yourself back to peace is something you *always* want to prioritize. You can still practice the forgiveness process even when you don't feel at peace because your intention is what really counts. As fear diminishes, the Holy Spirit can then do the necessary work by removing the guilt that is causing the blocks to your awareness of love's presence.

All you need to do is *trust* that the work is being done *without* your interference. What I mean by that is, without you needing to analyze or figure out anything. That's the beauty of letting go. The work is being done *behind* the scenes by the One Who can do it. From that space of peace, realizing that you are not your body, and being okay with what appears, you then take whatever form of action you may feel inspired to take. That puts you at the *cause* of healing as opposed to the *effect* of the illusion of sickness. And most importantly helps eliminate suffering.

Let me share an example of what I would say in a situation like that. When any sign of fear arises I would say;

> *"Dear Holy Spirit, please reinterpret this experience for me, for all I want is to experience peace. I don't know what it means, only You know. I release to You all judgments and interpretations. I trust that whatever needs to be done You'll take care of it, and whatever You guide me to do I'll do. Trusting Your loving guidance and wisdom, I release my thoughts to You and I give thanks, and so it is, Amen."*

Please pay close attention to what I am about to say. First of all, notice that I did *not* ask for healing. I did not ask for a particular condition to be removed, because the thing to remember is that *there is no condition*. If I ask to be healed from a particular condition, all I am doing is *assuming* that the condition *exists*, therefore *making it real to me.*

It does not matter what your eyes see or the body feels because it's all an illusion. By offering the illusion to the Holy Spirit for reinterpretation, all you are doing is *undoing* the part of you, the false-self that projected the illusion in the first place. You are asking for *True* vision, for *right-mindedness*; putting you in a very *peaceful* state of mind. A state where there is no more suffering, which also gives you access to *clarity*. From that space not only is true healing most likely to occur, but you are also *accelerating* your awakening process.

A Course in Miracles reminds me: *"Sickness is a decision. It is not a thing that happens to you, quite unsought, which makes you weak and brings you suffering.* **It is a choice you make, a plan you lay, when for an instant truth arises in our own deluded mind**, *and all your world appears to totter and prepare to fall."* **W-pI.136.7:1-3** In other words, when the truth of Who you are, which is perfect oneness with God arises, since the ego mind is the one projecting all your illusions, the illusion of illness is experienced in order for the ego to *protect itself* from the truth. This is when you are given an opportunity to *choose* between the ego or the Holy Spirit's thought system. By choosing the ego as your guide, sickness becomes your decision. By choosing the Holy Spirit on the other hand, through choosing peace first, and *practicing* forgiveness, you are allowing the truth of *Who you really are* to clear up your deluded mind from all thoughts of sickness. Remember once again that you are *not* healing a body, what you are healing is the mind, one that is split between two different thought systems. The Holy Spirit is helping us unify our thinking, by removing the blocks to the awareness of love's presence. Or we could say, removing the blocks to the awareness of our True Self, which is perfect, whole, and complete.

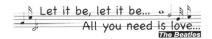

Let it be, let it be...
All you need is love....
The Beatles

XII
Wealth & Abundance

"The Father has given you all that is His, and He Himself is yours with them."
-A Course in Miracles [Text: chapter 11, section VI, paragraph 6, sentence 6]

"And he said unto him, Son, thou art ever with me, and all that I have is thine."
-Bible [Luke: chapter 15, verse 31]

When people talk about wealth and abundance, for the most part they think of one thing and one thing only, *money*. Yet, if *Who you are* is already abundant, what you are lacking is not money but the *experience* of your abundance. From that experience, whatever it is that resembles abundance shows up in your life. However, the ego being very insidious will always find ways to make you feel anything less than abundant regardless of how much you have or don't have.

Wealth and abundance is a state of consciousness. There have been times when I had money and did not feel abundant, and yet, during the writing of this book, I have been broke yet able to walk through the park and experience abundance. From that space, situations presented themselves that supported me as I continued to do what I was *inspired* to do. So while the ego was screaming at me, asking me to go out there and do whatever it takes to bring in money, my Spirit would say, *be still*. And in the midst of my experience, an overwhelming feeling of peace would take over. From that space, I receive guidance as to what my next step should be.

That being said, since I know money is a big issue for most, I would like to share what the real meaning of financial freedom is by first sharing what it is *not*. Financial freedom is *not* the idea that if you accumulate money you can then have the freedom to do what you want, that's the power people give to money; it's not the right idea, because money is not real in the first place.

Remember that anything you give power to in this world of illusion becomes your god. *A Course in Miracles* reminds me: *"But have no other gods before Him or you will not hear. God is not jealous of the gods you make, but you are. You would save them and serve them, because you believe that they made you. You think they are your father, because you are projecting onto them the fearful fact that you made them to replace God. Yet when they seem to speak to you, remember that nothing can replace God, and whatever replacements you have attempted are nothing."* T-10.III.8.:3-7 *"Thou shalt have no other gods before me."* [Exodus:20:3]

Before continuing with this chapter, I am going to make a very radical statement. It is *impossible* to experience real abundance because the world we seem to be living in was projected for the sole purpose of experience the opposite of abundance. Abundance in a true sense if our experience of the Kingdom, where we are One with all!

Our physical experience, being one of separation, all we experience is scarcity, even if we had a billion dollars in the back because this world is made out of fear. That's why *A Course in Miracles* reminds me, *"The dreams you think you like would hold you back as much as those in which the fear is seen. For every dream is but a dream of fear, no matter what the form it seems to take. The fear is seen within, without, or both. Or it can be disguised in pleasant form. But never is it absent from the dream, for fear is the material of dreams, from which they all are made."* T-29.IV.2:1-5

Having said that, writing a chapter on wealth an abundance in a world that was made to represent the opposite of oneness could be considered like an oxymoron. However, as I continue to share my present understanding of the course's teachings as well as my personal experiences, not to be mistaken by having anything to do with Truth, for Truth is not of this world, I will openly share events that have taken place in my life as I continue on this path of healing the mind.

Speaking strictly in dualistic terms, true financial freedom is the *knowing* that whenever a desired experience that may require an investment in the form of money need to take place, the amount needed to take care of it *will be there*. At least, I can honestly say that that has been my personal experience.

Most people seek money or whatever material things they want in order to feel abundant. Spirit asks us to simply recognize our abundance in the *midst* of whatever experience we are having. The reason being is that if we are *judging* our experiences, all we are doing is making them *seem* real. If I look at my experience, especially as I am writing this book, my abundance has nothing to do with how much I have in the bank; it has to do with *the way I am being mysteriously supported* as I continue on my journey. I must say, that's how faith is developed. The opportunity is being given for me to forgive everything I see that is *not* aligned with my True Self.

But how do you have the experience of remembering Who you are when your experience shows you the opposite? Like everything else, by recognizing that it is all an illusion and by allowing the Holy Spirit to remove all the guilt that is in your unconscious mind by applying the forgiveness process. In my case, for example, whenever I found myself dealing with a circumstance or condition, especially in the areas of wealth and abundance that triggered me to apply the forgiveness process, I would take a deep breath and say something along the lines of:

> "*Beloved Holy Spirit, please remove these discomforting feelings and reinterpret them for me. I release them to You, knowing that by aligning my thoughts with Yours my peace is restored. I forgive myself, and I thank You God for this awareness and I release all concerns to You in exchange for my peace, and so it is. Amen.*"

Notice that I am *not* asking for *specifics* such as more money, a bigger house, enough to pay my rent, etc. All I am asking for is *first* and *foremost peace of mind*, and then for the experience of abundance *trusting* that the Holy Spirit will choose whatever experience would be the perfect one for me. What is the point of getting what we want, if we are then fearful of loosing it? If my peace of mind is at stake, then there is a reason why I may not be getting what I thought would make me happy.

And by the way, all that we desire is God, right-mindedness (peace). Everything else is just details, illusions. And what is The Course asking us to do? It is asking us to choose God instead of our illusions.

I was having a conversation with a friend last night and I shared how I would respond if someone said to me, "*I am about to lose my house, or my relationship or this or that!*" My answer is always the same, "*So what seems to be the problem?*" They see the problem as losing things while I see the problem as losing their peace of mind. We *must* remember that **you are better off losing everything while having your peace of mind, than having everything at the expense of losing your peace of mind.** The question that arises now is, can I have both, what I want and peace of mind? The answer would be yes, as long as you are *not attached* to what you want.

From that place of peace, where you know you are truly supported by Spirit, ideas may emerge that may be the solution to your seeming problems. Also, because of your detachment and trust, you are likely to have fun, exciting, and incredible experiences that will not get in the way of your awakening process. An example would be Eckhart Tolle, the author of *The Power of Now* and *The New Earth*. In that same conversation I was having with my friend, when Eckhart's name came up my friend said to me, "*Yes, look at* Eckhart's *story. He was in parks just being and now he made it to the Oprah Show. Without trying to make anything happen, he finally made it!*" At that moment I said to my friend that he just missed the mark. The ego would make you believe that Eckhart's made it by being on Oprah's show. The reality is, *he made it the moment he became aware* of *Who he really is.* He made it the moment he found himself in those parks having an *awareness* of his True Self, even while he was having the experience of being broke. Now he may have lots of money, but his abundance has *nothing* to do with what he has, because he is at peace and completely *detached* from all his possessions. And the fact that he is so detached, he is now in a much better position to *enjoy* the things he has acquired, plus the experiences that are taking place in his life.

I am going to share an illusion around money that took place in my life, just to give you an idea as to how things can arrange themselves in order to bring forth a desire that may be rising within you. Keep in mind however that all our worldly desires are of the ego because a body cannot have desire of its own. Only a mind that believes it is a body experiences what appear to be corporal desires.

Around July 2005, I attended a seminar in the beautiful mountains of California. I flew out a few days early to spend a little time in what I knew was going to be my home for the second time. I visited my cousin and some friends. I drove through San Diego, and even when I did not see where I intended to live, I just knew that I wanted to relocate there. I had no clue about how I would support myself once I relocated. All I had in the bank was enough to cover living expenses for maybe three months, hoping no unexpected surprises would show up.

After attending the seminar, right there and then, my decision to move solidified in my gut. Before moving to California, I had only one week to pack, I also had two comedy engagements on the east coast. So I had to keep in mind that from California the traveling expenses to the east coast are higher. While living in Florida, my only traveling expense was gasoline. Now, I needed to add airfare, car rental and gasoline.

I am going to share the sequence of events that took place right after that seminar. My flight back to Florida was delayed; this in turn, caused me to miss my connecting flight. The airline offered to fly me on an alternate route that would include an overnight flight. I asked if they could just put me in a hotel for the evening and I would pick up the next morning flight. They gratefully accepted my request and gave me a few vouchers for meals. The next morning my flight was overbooked. I volunteered my seat and received a $200 flight voucher. The next flight was also overbooked and I received a $400 voucher. The next one was also overbooked. I ended up receiving a total of $1,000 in flying vouchers and the airline paid for another night at the hotel with more meal vouchers. The $1,000 worth of travel vouchers would take care of all flying expenses for my upcoming comedy engagements across the country.

On my way home from the airport, I stopped to pick up my mail. Inside was a letter from an investment group asking me if I was willing to sell my piece of land that I owned in Florida. The land was going to be auctioned by the state because the taxes were not paid. Let me give you a little history on that property. I inherited the piece of land from my Grandmother back in the early 90's. Around 1997, I was homeless and filed for bankruptcy. I gave the property to the county because I could not pay the taxes. End of story right? *Eight years later*, just a week before I would move to California, after I received $1,000 worth of travel vouchers, I get this letter, *not* from the state, but from an independent company who tracked me down, God knows how, with an offer to pay my back taxes while also giving me $5,000 for the property.

First, I was taken a little bit by surprise. I thought this must be some kind of a joke. The county's last address for me was in West Los Angeles, California dating back to 1997. Second, I started to wonder why someone would want to offer me $5,000 in cash for that lot. I called the county office with the lot number and all the information regarding the property contained in the letter sent to me by the investment company. The county office told me that the lot was still under my name and that it would go to a tax auction in the next two weeks! That is *eight years after* surrendering it to the county.

I asked what the tax debt was and they said $901.00. I went ahead and paid it on the spot! Then I contacted a few real estate agents in the local area in order to find out the current market value of the property. Are you ready for this? The actual fair market value was $47,000. About a month later, while I was fulfilling one of my comedy engagements, the property was sold. As you can see, I listened to what I was guided to do, and the resources presented *themselves* as a means of supporting me on my journey. Please keep in mind that this example is *not* meant for you to think that you should start setting up goals in order to try and change the illusion to fit your idea of what your life should be about. You will find many spiritual and motivational teachers quote, and misinterpret *A Course in Miracles'* teachings in order to fit their *individual agendas.*

Remember, all I shared with you, as exciting as it may seem, cannot even compare to the experience one has after the illusion of separation is restored. By simply giving your thoughts and judgments to the Holy Spirit while allowing Him to guide you as you awaken from this dream, you open yourself up to experiences that can be far more impressive than the illusion I just shared. And by the way, I am not implying that you should sit at home, do nothing, and just wait for the money or the opportunities to show up. I simply said, do nothing and *listen.* Listen does not mean sitting in front of the television or reading a mystery novel. I am talking about communing with your Inner Guide thru peace. And from that space you'll be guided as to what to do. And if you don't know what that is, just do whatever you *feel* you need to do *anyway.* The time will come when you'll feel more comfortable listening as your trust develops. It takes *practice.*

For example, I did not feel like getting a job when I thought I needed one the most. Not because it matter but because as I look back I can see that it would not have been the right decision for me at that moment. Ironically, that gave me all the time I needed to deepen my spiritual practice and study *A Course in Miracles,* resulting in me being able to write this book. Whatever you are guided to do in order to experience your abundance, which is not of this world anyway, follow it; whether it comes in the form of a hunch, a vision, an intuitive feeling or however, it *must* be followed, just don't make the mistake of making it important for nothing in a world of illusion can have any meaning.

To most, listening to their Inner Guidance is the hardest part. because in many cases that guidance seems to contradict *every single thought* they hold to be true. Besides, how could anyone trust their Inner Guidance? Since everything we've been taught since childhood is to listen to everyone else, to look for the answers outside, to rely on the "experts", "gurus" "authority" figures, on seeming "facts", worst, on our "experience". That's why it helps when *A Course in Miracles* reminds me: *"Listen and do not question what you hear for God does not deceive. He would have you replace the ego's belief in littleness with His Own exalted Answer to what you are so that you can cease to question it and know it for what it is."* **T-9.VIII.11:8-9**

As you continue to practice forgiveness, you are simply opening to the *experience* of what *A Course in Miracles* refers to as *The Happy Dream*; where you will experience pure joy and happiness as you are awakening from the dream no matter what it is you are doing. In other words, you *do not* have to be enlightened before having this happy dream experience, all you need is to be *willing* to listen to the One Who can guide you. *A Course in Miracles* reminds me: *"Rest in the Holy Spirit, and allow His gentle dreams to take the place of those you dreamed in terror and in fear of death. He brings forgiving dreams, in which the choice is not who is the murderer and who shall be the victim. In the dreams He brings there is no murder and there is no death. The dream of guilt is fading from your sight, **although your eyes are closed. A smile has come to lighten up your sleeping face. The sleep is peaceful now, for these are happy dreams.**"* **T-27.VII.14:3-8**

Does that mean I cannot ask for what I want, you may ask? It's not a question of whether you can ask for what you want. It is that we do not know what we want. That's why *A Course in Miracles* reminds me, "*Your function here is only to decide against deciding what you want, in recognition that you do not know*." **T-14.IV.5:2**

That being said, remember that whatever it is you want, whether it is coming from fear or trust, if it has to do with this world, it is not real. It is a false idol. From *The Disappearance of the Universe,* by Gary Renard, Pursah said to Gary:

"*...most people don't want to hear that their dreams and passions are really false idols—a substitute for God and Heaven.*"

Then goes on to say:

"*There is nothing wrong with your dream if you understand it and forgive it. Forgive—and then do what you and the Holy Spirit choose to, and have fun!*"

I have been asked, what is it that I want, and my response is peace. Because I realize that in wanting peace, I open myself to having *everything*. In the process of wanting peace more than anything else, I find myself trusting more, being more creative. From that space I am led to write this book among other things, and most importantly, I have the *experience* of being *fully* supported throughout the process. That allows me to continue building *faith* and *trust*.

Keep practicing your forgiveness process and let the Holy Spirit guide you through peace. God is never leading you to poverty, *you are*. God is trying to lead you to the kingdom. *A Course in Miracles* reminds me: *"If God's Will for you is complete peace and joy, unless you experience only this* **you must be refusing to acknowledge His Will**. *His Will does not vacillate, being changeless forever. When you are not at peace it can only be because* **you do not believe you are in Him**. *Yet His is All in all."* **T-8.IV.1:1-4**

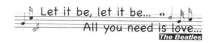
The Beatles

XIII
Career

"All real pleasure comes from doing God's Will. This is because not doing it is a denial of Self."
-A Course in Miracles [Text: chapter 1, section VII, paragraph 1, sentence 4, 5]

"I delight to do thy will, O my God: yea, thy law is within my heart."
-Bible [Psalms: Psalm 40, verse 8]

When most people talk about career, they usually mean the work they'll be doing in order to generate income. They equate the word career with work. Some start their own business, others get a college education and some just end up being trained and employed by an independent company. Even those who receive a formal education, most of the time the reason why they chose a particular career is because of the financial earning potential and/or the so called "prestige" of their chosen occupation.

Regardless of the reason(s) why most people choose their line of work, if their decision is based on external influences such as prestige, the money they can make, pressure from family or friends, that decision was made out of fear. Some may even develop diseases just by not being able to cope with their choice of career. Now, in a script that is already written, there is not much we can do about our circumstances, unless through practicing forgiveness and the collapsing of time, an exchange of illusions could take place.

But since we are dealing with our physical experience, which even though it is not real, it is however our experience, a peaceful frame of mind allows us to perceive differently, and experiences such as the following could take place in our life. Here is a story told by a wonderful physician, Dr. Bernie S. Siegel, M.D., which although in Truth is not real, makes it for a very inspiring and happy anecdote. The story is about an individual whose passion was to play the violin. Upon graduation his parents suggested that he attend law school since they believed that playing the violin was no way to make a living. As an attorney he had a very good practice but unfulfilling. He was diagnosed with cancer of the brain and was told by his doctors that he had only about a year to live. After being diagnosed he decided to pick up his violin and at least spend his last days doing something he *loved* so much. A year later, he was giving a concert with his violin and the cancer *disappeared* completely!

The purpose of the story is not for you to believe in it as being real; it is to make a point. The reason most people make decisions based on fear is because they simply don't know how to *trust*. Trust what? Trust *their inner Guidance*. When we are asked to let go and let God, we are asked to listen to our spiritual guidance *regardless* of logic.

From the Manual for Teachers' section, *A Course in Miracles* reminds me: *"A major hindrance in this aspect of his learning is the teacher of God's fear about the validity of what he hears. And what he hears **may indeed be quite startling**. It may also seem to be quite irrelevant to the presented problem as he perceives it, and may, in fact, confront the teacher with a situation that appears to be very embarrassing to him."* M-21.5:1-3 A few sentences up, The Course says: *"Judge not the words that come to you, but offer them in confidence. **They are far wiser than your own.**"* M-21.5:6-7

To share a dualistic anecdote from my life as an example, as a very young child I loved to teach, to help others and I guess I wanted to be popular. That last part never seemed to happen. I was, and still am very creative and artistically talented. When I picked up my first guitar around the age of eleven or twelve, I spent hours on end playing and thinking that my passion was to become a musician; that faded away. When I moved to Florida, I took flying lessons, thinking I wanted to be a commercial pilot like my cousin; that faded away also. Then a passion for comedy took over and for more than ten years I made my living as a stand-up comedian. Then the desire to write and produce music resurfaced and I ended up having a recording studio and even produced songs for artists. And although many of the things I did were very exciting at the time, they never brought me *permanent* fulfillment. Interestingly enough, what I am doing right this moment, writing this book and sharing these principles with you is one of the *most* fulfilling things I have ever done. Clearly since the mid-1980s, this is something I have been drawn to more than anything else, but I kept ignoring it, because I thought I knew what I wanted.

So, you may ask; *How do I find a fulfilling career?* Like everything else, it is not something you find or search for, it is something you *allow* to emerge through you as the Holy Spirit removes any obstacles to your perception. And you don't have to quit everything you are doing right now, but at least you can start noticing what seems to bring you joy, regardless of how absurd it may seem. And when you find yourself moving in that direction and fear comes up, you practice your forgiveness process.

Remember that when you are letting go, you are now becoming a vehicle available for God to use you. Keep in mind that as you move in the direction of whatever you feel guided to do, *always practice detachment*. Otherwise you will not be able to listen to your inner guidance, for the ego has turned your passion into a false idol. So even though what I am doing right now may seem like something worthy to share, it is still an illusion. *Nothing* of this world is important. If this book turns me into an international author, speaking worldwide, I have to continue to remember that my purpose here is *my salvation, my awakening* from this dream.

So how do we apply the forgiveness process when it comes to our career? For me, I would say that I would ask mostly for clarity and correction of perception. I would say something along these lines:

> *"Holy Spirit, I forgive myself and surrender to You these feelings of seeming confusion for I know that I must not be trusting. I ask for guidance and strength as I remind myself of Who I am through doing God's Will. Please use me in a way that I can serve You as I continue to awaken from this dream. Let my career be one through which I only do Your Will. Please help me restore my peace of mind so that my vision is restored. With peace in my heart I say thanks Holy Spirit and so it is. Amen."*

What am I asking for? Peace and strength as I am developing trust, while also offering the discomforting feelings to the Holy Spirit for reinterpretation. After my forgiveness prayer, I just go on with my life doing whatever it is that I'm doing, and if there is something I need to know, I know it will be clearly revealed to me. It takes practice to learn how to differentiate between the ego and the Holy Spirit's peaceful guidance. Yet the Holy Spirit asks for one thing only, your *willingness to practice listening*. Not sometimes, but *all the time.*

By a mere shift in awareness as a result of doing your practices, your current career could turn into a very fulfilling one. And if that is not the one for you, at least you will make the best out of it as you are being prepared for your awakening process, which will come about as a result of the collapsing of time, not as an exchange of illusions in order to make your world real, because remember that the Holy Spirit is not interested in what you do for a living, rather in knowing that you are not attached to anything of this world. After that, whatever you end up ding is just that, stuff you do in the world.

In closing this chapter, I would like to share an interesting illusion, that although it is not real, I think you'll enjoy. When I was working at a music store, just before starting to write this book, I had many reasons to feel uncomfortable, obviously because that is how it was all set up according to the script, given the fact that it is a projection, but anyway, the music was loud, plus the kind of music that was played could be considered very negative. Also most of the employees did not have anywhere near the type of mentality we are talking about in this book.

However, as I kept practicing my forgiveness process things mysteriously began to change, not that that's why I was doing it, yet, the first thing that changed was the way *I* started to perceived my working environment. And that's really the key, a change in perception not a change in circumstances. Interestingly enough, not that it matters, but the company changed the rules about the kind of music being played, making it more customer friendly. Also the speakers in the department I was working in were removed, making the environment quieter and peaceful. Some employees who were very negative were asked to leave, while the ones I did not resonate with became friendlier. Ironically, all these changes started to take place just when I gave my two-weeks notice. However, that's okay, because the time for me to write this book came next.

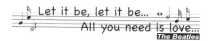

XIV
Feelings & Emotions

"If you are afraid, you will inevitably value wrongly, and by endowing all thoughts with equal power will inevitably destroy peace. That is why the Bible speaks of 'the peace of God which passeth understanding'. This peace is totally incapable of being shaken by errors of any kind. It denies the ability of anything not of God to affect you."
-A Course in Miracles [Text: chapter 2, section II, paragraph 1, sentence 7 - 11]

"And the peace of God, which passeth all understanding, shall keep your hearts and minds through Christ Jesus."
-Bible [Philippians: chapter 4, verse 7]

Dealing with feelings and emotions is probably one of the most challenging things to forgive because they are right in our face. It is easy to understand intellectually the forgiveness process and apply it, but when our feelings and emotions become disturbed, all we want is release from them as *fast* as we can. Although we could go on forever analyzing our feelings and emotions to death, just like every other area of our lives, the process of releasing the guilt behind what we are feeling is the same.

There are lots of very well meaning teachers who suggest that the quality of our life is determined by the quality of our emotions, when the truth is, the quality of our life is determined by our *ability* to experience peace *regardless* of what is going on with our emotions. Just ask people who have it all, who are either coming in and out of rehabilitation clinics or dealing with severe emotional pain, what would they rather have? Do you think they would rather have pleasure or to be at peace? One example out of many is a comedian knew who in my opinion had the most brilliant comedy mind in history. He went to a seminar by a very well known teacher and was given the "tools" on how to manage his emotions, pretty much like every other attendee. In 2007, in the midst of the height of his career, he put a gun in his mouth and committed suicide. Let me ask you, at that moment, what do you think he wanted more than ever, to learn how to manage his emotions, or as some may say his "states", or to be at peace? I guess it doesn't take a brain surgeon to figure out the answer. You play with your emotions and you are playing with fire. In other words, you choose the ego as your savior, and that's what you set yourself up for.

We must remember that our feelings and emotions are *not* telling us what is real, they are simply making us *believe* that what we feel is real, therefore grounding us to the body. In other words, they solidify the illusion that the body is real. I would like to share a personal experience. I was staying at my girlfriend's house and this overwhelming feeling of sadness and guilt took over my being. I did not know where it came from; all I knew was that it was there. At that moment, with tears rolling down my face, I offered the feelings to the Holy Spirit, and while I was feeling them, I continued to forgive myself for what I was experiencing. In about an hour, my girlfriend came back from work and the guilt feelings were gone. To this day, I don't know what they meant or what they were about. All I know is that those feelings disappeared.

I would like to share two additional examples before continuing. Practitioner Ron D. Blair shared at group about a time when he found himself in the fetal position, laying on his bed, not even having the will to get up. All he could do was to practice forgiveness, even when he did not know what he was forgiving. A few days went by until his experience began to change. To this day, all he knows is that an inner transformation took place.

The second example is the one of Nouk Sanchez, co-author of *Take Me To Truth, Undoing the Ego*, where she shares of a time when she experienced severe depression. It went on for a significant period of time, to the point where doctors started to show extreme concern. However, having studied The Course for a number of years, somewhere deep within, she knew what was going on. The ego was simply being gradually undone. After her experience, and being able to fully recover as a result of practicing forgiveness, she facilitates talks and workshops worldwide along with her co-author Tomas Vieira, in order to bring awareness to those who find themselves dealing with similar experiences. That's why *A Course in Miracles* reminds me, *"I need do nothing."* **T-18.VII** Meaning that there is nothing for me to fix, or change, or do, all that is required of me is to release, to surrender, not to resist, to trust, to let go.

When offering your feelings and emotions for forgiveness, there may be times when an insight may be revealed to you, yet many times the feelings will dissipate *without* you ever knowing what they meant or where they came from. The Holy Spirit works *behind the scenes*, doing the cleaning. All we need to do is to keep the door open, so like a cleaning crew, it can get in and do the cleaning. Always remember that whatever it is you are forgiving, peace of mind is what you are *really* trying to obtain, *not* answers. Using the cleaning crew analogy, they will do the work in your house; you don't even have to be there. However, they can't get in unless *you* open the door. Your forgiveness process is your willingness to open the door. Your *trust* is in leaving the house, letting the crew do the work *without* your interference.

Before sharing a forgiveness process just like I have shared with you in each chapter, let's talk for a moment about the good feelings and emotions. Remember that the goal is not to feel good, but to awaken from this dream by remembering that it is *all* an illusion. So if you are feeling good about something, appreciate the feeling, enjoy whatever is taking place in a non-attached manner, while offering all those great feelings to God also. Because the ego is always trying to get your attention in whatever way it can. If it cannot get your attention through you feeling bad (pain), it will do so by projecting the transitory illusion of feeling good (pleasure). *A Course in Miracles* reminds me: *"Pain demonstrates the body must be real. It is a loud, obscuring voice whose shrieks would silence what the Holy Spirit says, and keep His words from your awareness. Pain compels attention, drawing it away from Him and focusing upon itself.* **Its purpose is the same as pleasure, for they both are means to make the body real.***"* T-27.VI.1:1-4

Most people have the tendency to equate feeling good, miracles, and healings with getting what they want; only to find the good feeling and all that it denotes is only *transitory*. Keep in mind that feeling good convinces us that our body is real, and that the *most important* goal of the ego is to *ensure* that we *believe* we are first and foremost bodies having a physical experience *separate* from our Source, from God. Once that belief has been established, the ego can then launch its merciless attack.

So in giving our concerns to the Holy Spirit, and making peace our *most important* priority, we receive a great sense of joy that is beyond what we can manage to accomplish. This joy is *not* a feeling we go after when we are allowing the Holy Spirit to do the work for us, but what is *revealed* through us *naturally* as the blocks to the awareness of love's presence are being removed from our consciousness. *A Course in Miracles* reminds me: *"The dreams you think you like would hold you back as much as those in which the fear is seen. For* **every dream** *is but a dream of fear,* **no matter** *what the form it seems to take. The fear is seen within, without, or both.* **Or it can be disguised in pleasant form.** *But never is it absent from the dream, for fear is the material of dreams, from* **which they all are made.***"* T-29.IV.2:1-5

Our work is to move from a transient world to a *permanent* one; away from the world where feeling good only lasts a little while, to the *permanency* of Heaven where there is *only* joy, happiness, love, fulfillment and peace. So if you feel depressed, you don't want to get rid of depression, you want to experience your joy, you don't want to get rid of sadness, you want to experience your happiness, you don't want to get rid of the pain, you want to experience the guiltless mind that could not experience pain. That's what happens when you remember *Who you really are*. So if I were to find myself dealing with an emotional issue, here is what I would say:

> *"Holy Spirit, I don't know what this means and it is not important either. I just want you to help bring myself back to peace. I choose peace now with Your help Holy Spirit, I forgive myself and I offer my thoughts to You, knowing that You know what is best. I now choose peace and so it is. Amen."*

As with every situation or circumstance, all I am asking for is peace and guidance, *not* specifics. From that point I simply trust that the work is being done. And if the feeling persists, I continue practicing the forgiveness process for as long as I feel the need. In some cases, there are so many layers of ego and guilt that it seems as if the forgiveness process may go on forever. I can assure you, however, at least from my own experience, that the work is being done. And like with health and healing, if there is anything you feel moved to do in order to help you alleviate the pain, then you do so.

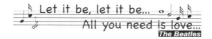

Let it be, let it be...
All you need is love...
The Beatles

XV
Helping Others & The World

"Of your ego you can do nothing to save yourself or others, but of your spirit you can do everything for the salvation of both."
-A Course in Miracles [Text: chapter 4, section I, paragraph 12, sentence 1]

"Verily, verily, I say unto you, The Son can do nothing of himself, but what he seeth the Father do: for what things soever he doeth, these also doeth the Son likewise."
-Bible [John: chapter 5, verse 19]

A *Course in Miracles* reminds me: *"Damnation is your judgment on yourself, and this you will project upon the world. **See it as damned**, and all you see is **what you did** to hurt the Son of God. If you behold disaster and catastrophe, you tried to crucify him. If you see holiness and hope, you joined the Will of God*

161

to set him free. There is no choice that lies between these two decisions." T-21.in.2:1-5

Unlike many scriptures that seem to be filled with contradictions, one thing about The Course is that it is very clear when it says that the world is an illusion; that it is a figment of our imagination and that everything we see is a projection from within. *A Course in Miracles* reminds me: *"**There is no world!** This is the central thought The Course attempts to teach. Not everyone is ready to accept it, and each one must go as far as he can let himself be led along the road to truth."* W-pI.132.6:2-4

A Course in Miracles also reminds us that we are all one. Therefore, whatever we seem to see outside of ourselves is really nothing but an outside projection of an inner idea we hold as true; an illusion projected by the ego in order to make us believe that we are separate. So if what we see outside is a projection of what's really going on inside our own awareness, then who are those in need? Are they real or are they projections of what we believe to be true? So how do we help those who seem to be in need if they are really illusions?

I will be very *cautious* in answering that question because I don't want you to think that I am not compassionate or loving. First we must understand that an illusion is simply a projection that is reflecting back at us our present level of consciousness, it is simply projecting outward the guilt that is hidden deep within our unconscious. That being the case, if we see someone as guilty for example, that means that *we* are guilty. If we perceive someone as being powerless, then what we are saying is that either we are powerless or that we believe in the concept of powerlessness. And that is why we are projecting out onto the screen of our consciousness the *belief* that manifests itself as reality in this illusion we call our physical world.

So when I project the illusion of people being let's say homeless, hungry, sick, or whatever the illusion may seem, including when I feel inclined to offer them some assistance, I use that opportunity to see the power and greatness of God *within them,* not as bodies, but as essence. And by me being able to see them as *Who they really are, perfect, whole* and *complete, without* any pity, judgment or sense of guilt, I am actually reminding *myself* of *my own* perfection, wholeness and completeness, therefore helping us *both* remember. *A Course in Miracles* reminds me: *"He is the frame in which your holiness is set, and what God gave him must be given you. However much he overlooks the masterpiece in him and sees only a frame of darkness,* **it is still your only function to behold in him what he sees not.***"* T-25.II.8:6-7

I want you to please pay close attention to the last sentence: *"However much he overlooks the masterpiece in him and sees only a frame of darkness,* **it is still your only function** *to behold in him what he sees not."* The masterpiece he overlooks is his True Self. My function is to behold in him what he sees not. But here is the catch. If I see in him anything less than perfection, that means I have already seen the imperfection in me first. That being the case, I have actually *overlooked* the masterpiece in *me*. The ego simply projected him as my excuse for me not to acknowledge *my own* seeming imperfection, so that I can see it somewhere else. Needless to say, as long as the guilt remains in me, and not allowing the thought system of the Holy Spirit change my perception, I will continue to project it outwards, therefore seeing a world filled with *imperfection*.

Before continuing, here is where we need to be careful. The world of illusion will *always* be seen as imperfect because it represent the belief in separation. So there is really no hope for this world. However, the forgiveness process allows us to overlook illusions so that we don't find ourselves being affected by what the eyes seem to see. So it is not what we see but our *interpretation* of what we think we see that is corrected through the forgiveness process, therefore allowing us to experience the peace that passes understanding.

On a broader scale such as world hunger or war, the same principle applies. Since what we are seeing is a projection of our inner awareness, while we may feel inspired to help and give support, we *must* continue *practicing* forgiveness and inner peace. For once we have accepted them for ourselves, we are then more likely to see a world that would reflect our new way of being. *A Course in Miracles'* Manual for Teachers reminds me: *"Peace is* **impossible** *to those who look on war. Peace is* **inevitable** *to those who* **offer** *peace. How easily, then, is your judgment of the world escaped! It is* **not** *the world that makes peace seem impossible. It is the world* **you see** *that* **is** *impossible."* M-11.4:1-4

Yes, it is nice to help, but if we try to do it at the level of the illusion, *without* changing our *mind* through forgiveness, it is like trying to rearrange the chairs on a sinking ship as opposed to leaving the ship. In other words, it is like trying to *rearrange* the *dream*, or in this case the nightmare, as opposed to *awakening* from it, which is what The Course is leading us to. The Course is *not* interested in *fixing* anything, *we* are the ones trying to fix things.

So while we may feel inspired to do something to help, which is a wonderful way of sharing our love, let's remember what is *really* taking place. We are being given an opportunity to see the conflict we hold *within ourselves*, so that we can heal it through forgiveness.

So, how can we apply forgiveness while seeing people in need, suffering or nations at war? What I do is, I notice how I feel when I see the images presented on the screen of my conscious awareness. If I see someone who is in seeming distress for example, and it triggers any discomforting feelings, at that moment I am given an opportunity to practice forgiveness. I may say something like:

> *"I see God in you. I see your perfection. I forgive myself for projecting what I see, knowing that you are not really there. From this space of love, I ask the Holy Spirit to please reinterpret for me any feelings I have that are not aligned with my peace of mind. I see only love in you my brother because I know you are perfect, whole and complete, for you are God. I love you and I release any thoughts to the Holy Spirit so that I can see clearly, I am thankful and so it is. Amen."*

With anything that is happening globally, such as natural disasters, world war, etc., the same principle applies. After doing your forgiveness process, from that place of love, peace and forgiveness do what you feel inspired to do. If you want to send money, or food, or organize a group to assist, go do it. Not because you are fixing anything, but because you are making a statement of *Who you really are*. On the other hand, if you see others as victims, it means that you have bought into the illusion. There are no victims and no villains, only *you* caught in the midst of what could be considered an *unpleasant dream*.

As I bring this chapter to an end, I am going to share a statement that may be very challenging for many to accept, *especially* those who do not understand the nature of the ego or the principles taught in The Course. That statement is; **what the ego wants is for you to save the world.** The reason being is, as long as there is a physical world, where duality exist, there will *always* be hatred, anger, fear, greed, suffering, violence, and yes, we will experience the opposite as well because one cannot exist without the other. Still it all come back to the same statement, *there is no world!*

I like the way Liz Cronkhite founder of ACIMmentor.com puts it:

> "Whenever you 'read the signs' out there in the world - or even in just your own life - you are simply seeing the ego's interpretation that the world is real and meaningful. **You are perceiving nothing and interpreting it as something.** The Holy Spirit's interpretation of the world is always the same: The world is not real, so you do not have to interpret it, or give it meaning."

Joel L. Goldsmith reminds us from *The Infinite Way*:
"Because the human scene is entirely a misconception through misperception, any thought of helping, healing, correcting, or changing the material picture must be relinquished in order that we may see the ever-present Reality"

At times the Course employs strong language in order to make Its message clear. An example would be, *"This is an insane world, and do not underestimate the extent of its insanity."* **T-14.I.2:6,** Within the context of the Course's teachings the sentence could be changed to, *"This world is an illusion, and do not underestimate the power of its seeming reality."* Or *"This world is not your home, and do not underestimate your belief in thinking it is so."* Which by the way, *A Course in Miracles* reminds me: *"This world you seem to live in* **is not home to you.** *And somewhere in your mind* **you know that this is true."** W-pI.182.1:1-2 Bottom line is, choose God and you experience *Oneness*, choose the ego and you experience *the world*.

♪ Let it be, let it be... ♪
All you need is love...
The Beatles

XVI
Relationships

"There is no fear in perfect love because it knows no sin, and it must look on others as on itself."
-A Course in Miracles [Text: chapter 20, section III, paragraph 11, sentence 3]

"There is no fear in love; but perfect love casteth out fear: because fear hath torment. He that feareth is not made perfect in love."
-Bible [1 John: chapter 4, verse 18]

Through relationships we get to practice the *most* amount of forgiveness. You could say that it's the *superhighway* for undoing. They can make us or break us psychologically. Not because they have such power, but because we have unconsciously given them that power. We did so by attaching ourselves to them, making believe that they are the source of our love as opposed to our *Real* Source, which is God. Even when we experience all kinds of relationships, such as with co-workers, friends, close family, lovers, etc., I am going to briefly address love relationships in the romantic sense. Just like in every other example, the forgiving process is pretty much the same. Because whether it is a loving relationship, a career issue, money issue, or emotional issue, they are *all* illusions.

But what is the main difference between, let's say, a career issue and a human relationship issue? It's that humans can talk back to us. They can press our buttons far much faster and can hurt us deeper than any other issue we may have to face. So how do we deal with them? First I have to say that in the past, relationships have not been my strongest subject. I had to do a lot of healing, and still have some to do. Even to talk about relationships, especially after the recent one I had, in which we have become amazing friends and a great support to one another, all of this was possible because I applied the forgiveness process.

Nouk Sanchez and Tomas Vieira taught me something very powerful in their book, *Take Me To Truth Undoing The Ego*. And that was the understanding that when we are ready to let go, we never get what we want, we get what we *need* instead. Because when we are operating from ego, what is it that we want? We want our goals, our illusions. Yet, what is it that we need? We need to learn how to undo the ego through practicing patience, forgiveness, unconditional love, surrender and trust. People spend time trying to find the "right one" or their "soul-mate," just to find themselves disappointed and discouraged. They try everything, from seminars on relationships, love gurus, online dating, getting the right clothes, making the right moves, all in hopes that when the "one" shows up, they are prepared.

You hear a lot about relationship experts saying that you first have to learn to love yourself before you can love others. The problem is how can you love yourself if you *don't know* what love is. And what is The Course's goal? It is to help us *experience* love in a *Real* sense, which is our experience of our oneness with God, not something we seek for in this "world", specially since the world was projected for the sole purpose of not being able to experience true love but to experience separation. Only experiences of pleasure are what have been mistaken by thinking that they have anything to do with love. that's why *A Course in Miracles* clearly states in the introduction, "The course does not aim at teaching the meaning of love, **for that is** *beyond what can be taught. It does aim, however, at removing the blocks to the awareness of love's presence, which is your natural inheritance."* **T-In.1:6-7**

When Dawn and I met, there was really not much chemistry towards one another, but there was a deeper connection. She was dating, but never found anyone who was worth her time because she wanted something deeper. I also wanted someone who was very spiritual, but the problem was my ego wanted a woman with *specific* looks, especially since that is what most false idols teach; that you have to know what you want and write *specifically* what your "ideal mate" is supposed to look like and so on. Because of the work I have been doing, meaning, my forgiveness process, although I thought there was a particular type of woman I wanted, with Dawn I was given what I needed. In our relationship, I was able to experience the guilt I have felt in the past, but this time with someone who is patient, loving and understanding. And can you guess why she had those loving qualities? Because at a much deeper level, even without noticing it, *I* was the one becoming more patient, loving and understanding. Therefore she was simply reflecting back at me the qualities that I was starting to embrace for myself. Soon after we decided to end the form of the relationship, which goes to show you that not all relationships are meant to last forever in any one particular form, I met someone whom I was able to experience been loving *without* having to be attached to her. That does not mean that my new relationship did not bring new opportunities for me to practice forgiveness.

All I can say is that as a result of my forgiveness practice, I have come to the realization that I don't *need* to know what loving myself is, all I need to do is to *choose God first* and make God the *most important thing in my life,* and to remember that my love comes from God and *not* from anything or anyone in this world. The *simplicity* of the process is that I *don't have to figure anything out*. I just do the forgiveness process and the Holy Spirit takes care of the details. And with everything else, you don't do the forgiveness process in order to attract a mate because that is giving power to the illusion by wanting God to give you a symbol, an illusion, a false idol to fulfill an *illusionary* need. The forgiveness process is so that wherever guilt resides within your unconscious, it can be released so that you can experience a *more fulfilling, peaceful* and *happy* life as you awaken from this dream.

Loving in a Godlike manner does not require reciprocal love nor is it about giving, but more so about *extending* oneself. The love we receive from God is the extension of our oneness with all. When you extend your love, you want in your heart what is best for your beloved. When you give love, you just want love back, mostly because you *think* you need it, since you *forgot* you already are it. But the *truth* of what *real* love is can *only* be *experienced* when the blocks to the awareness of its presence are removed. That's *all* we are doing with the forgiveness process.

So what did I do when faced with challenging situations and seemingly apparent feelings of pain and discomfort that required forgiveness with my beloved? I said something like:

> *"Holy Spirit, I offer you these feelings of fear that I know are not part of Who I am and ask you to please reinterpret them for me, for I don't know what they mean and only You know. I forgive myself for having this feeling of discomfort around my girlfriend. So please help me bring myself back to peace. All I ask is for your peace Holy Sprit, and I thank you for this awareness and so it is. Amen."*

What am I doing? Asking for peace of mind and trusting that I did not know what these feelings meant, so I released them to the Holy Spirit to reinterpret them for me.

Simply remember that the fear of letting go is that you think you may not get what you want. I am here to say that at the beginning it may seem that way, because what you think you want may elude you, for the Holy Spirit is simply helping you strengthen your foundation. Once the foundation is strong by allowing God's will to be done, then you'll get what you *truly* desire. For you'll come to a very *profound realization*, which is, what Spirit wants for you and what you really want are *exactly* the same, *peace of mind*.

♪ Let it be, let it be... ♪
All you need is love...
The Beatles

XVII
True Forgiveness

"...forgive your brother, that the darkness may be lifted from your mind."
-A Course in Miracles [Text: chapter 29, section III, paragraph 4, sentence 2]

"Judge not, and ye shall not be judged: condemn not, and ye shall not be condemned: forgive, and ye shall be forgiven."
-Bible [Luke: chapter 6, verse 37]

A *Course in Miracles* reminds me: *"You think you hold against your brother what he has done to you. But what you really blame him for is for what **you did to him**. It is not his past but yours you hold against him. And you lack faith in him because of what you were. **Yet you are as innocent of what you were as he is.**"* T-17.VII.8:1-5

You may be wondering why I would want to write a chapter on forgiveness, when we have been talking about forgiveness throughout the book. The reason being is, forgiveness has been addressed mostly as a process and yes, although I have touched on the area of forgiveness from the illusory standpoint, I felt inspired to address forgiveness on a more personal level. I'll do so by comparing the way most people are taught to forgive as opposed to the way The Course addresses forgiveness. This time, as an example, I'll be using the illusion of someone doing something wrong to us. This could be a partner that cheated on us, a friend who betrayed us, a stranger who called us a name, vented angrily at us or someone who may have caused us either physical or emotional harm.

In a conventional way, forgiveness for most people, religions and society is based on the idea that someone has done something wrong and deserves to be forgiven. Yet what The Course says is that *nobody* has done anything wrong, the reason being is, there is really *nothing there to forgive* because if everything we see is a projection coming from within, then what we think is being done to us by someone else, is really being done to us *by* us. The Buddha said; *"You will not be punished for your anger, you'll be punished 'by' your anger."* I love the following words from Martha Lucía Espinosa's wonderful book titled *Spoken Miracles*;

> *"I had misunderstood the stormy nights that came forth after beginning my work with The Course as indicators of failure, when in reality they heralded the truth that I was really doing nothing more than learning how to **face the makings of my own ego**, and that's what needed to be healed."*

So when we see an illusion that seems to be treating us in ways where we feel like a victim, we must first understand that *we are* the ones projecting the illusion, we are ***facing the makings of our own ego***. From that point, instead of us trying to interpret the situation, we simply remember to forgive ourselves for what we have projected, and whatever discomfort we feel, offer it to the Holy Spirit for reinterpretation, for *only* then can true healing and peace of mind be experienced. *A Course in Miracles* reminds me: *"Forgiveness recognizes what you thought your brother did to you has not occurred.*

It does not pardon sins and make them real. It sees there was no sin. And in that view are all your sins forgiven." **W-pII.1.1:1-4**

I would like for you to pay attention to this line from the passage: *"It does not pardon sins and make them real."* Since nothing is real, there is nothing to pardon. By pardoning something is to make something real. The Course also says; *"Be willing to forgive the Son of God for what he did not do."* In forgiving the Son of God for what he did not do, you are forgiving *yourself* for what *you* did not do. For who is the Son of God? *You* are! Remember that we are all One and the Son and the Father are One. *"On that day you will realize that I am in my Father, and you are in me, and I am in you."* [**John 14:20**] Since there is no separation, everything you see is nothing more than an extension of *yourself*. A Course in Miracles reminds me: *"For no one in whom true forgiveness rests can suffer. He holds not the proof of sin before his brother's eyes. And thus he must have overlooked it and **removed it from his own**. Forgiveness cannot be for one and not the other. **Who forgives is healed**. And in his healing lies the proof that he has truly pardoned, and retains no trace of condemnation that he still would hold against himself or any living thing."* **T-27.II.3:6-11**

I find this line from The Course fascinating: *"Whom you forgive is given power to forgive you your illusions."* **T-29.III.3:12** The reason why the one you forgive has the power to forgive you your illusions is *not* because they have any power over you, but because *you* are now reclaiming *your own* power by realizing that they are *your* projection. All they are doing is showing you what *you* need to forgive so that you no longer have to project that guilt outward onto someone or something else. In releasing them you are actually releasing *yourself*. That's why The Course says; *"By your gift of freedom is it given unto you."* **T-29.III.3:13** I also love this line from *The Song of Prayer*, which is an extension of the principles of The Course where it says: *"It is **impossible to forgive another**, for it is **only your sins** you see in him. You want to see them there, and not in you. That's why **forgiveness of another is an illusion**."* **S-2.I.4:2-3**

I want to address one thing because after what I have just shared, I want to make sure you clearly understand that not only your brother is not guilty, but you aren't either. When I say that the one that is being forgiven is yourself, the ego then takes the guilt and projects it unto you. In other words, if you don't feel guilty for what you think someone has done to you, the ego then tries to make you believe that you are guilty for having projected the illusion. The beauty of the forgiveness process is that we are not the ones doing the work. The Holy Spirit is. By us giving up our thoughts to the Holy Spirit for reinterpretation, He is the one taking care of removing all the guilt that is in the mind.

At this point you may have some additional questions such as; *"But how do I know I am forgiving? How do I know I am doing it right? How am I supposed to feel when I forgive? How do I know this forgiveness process is working?"* I know I had some of the same questions. This is what's really taking place. Understanding that everything you see is nothing but illusions, and that they are ego's projections, by releasing your discomforting thoughts to the Holy Spirit you are doing the process correctly. Just by your *willingness* to forgive, that's *all* the Holy Spirit needs from you. The more you keep practicing the forgiveness process, you can rest assured that progress is being made. *A Course in Miracles* reminds me*:* **"Correction is not your function. It belongs to One Who knows of fairness, not of guilt. If you assume correction's role, you lose the function of forgiveness.** No one can forgive until he learns corrections is but to forgive, and never to accuse. **Alone you cannot see they are the same, and therefore is correction not of you**." T-27.II.10:1-5

So the two questions that have been answered so far are one, you are doing it right *no matter what* you may be experiencing and two, the Holy Spirit is doing the undoing of the ego for you. The next question is in regard to how you are supposed to feel while doing the forgiveness process. I have great news for you; if you happen to experience any particular feelings that would indicate that the process is working for you, that's fine. If not, that's okay too because as you keep doing the process, while *trusting* that the Holy Spirit is doing His part, the time comes when you no longer have the same feelings towards whatever illusion you may have projected, and the Course can be a bit disturbing because it will not let you off the hook. You must take *full responsibility* for *your* projections if you want to experience true healing. Make any kind of judgment towards anything or anyone and you have simply judged *yourself*.

So if I feel triggered by someone's behavior, while holding him/her/them (all being just really me of course) in my awareness, I would probably say something like:

> *"My beloved brother, I love you because I know you and I are one. Thank you for allowing me the opportunity to see an area in my life that needs to heal. Knowing that you are my own projection, I forgive myself for having made you up and forgive us both for what we have not done. Recognizing our innocence I release us both to the Holy Spirit. Thank you Holy Spirit for this awareness and please reinterpret any discomforting feelings for me for I don't know what they mean and only You do. From this place of love and forgiveness, I say Thank You God and so it is. Amen."*

Simply remember these words by Jesus the Christ, *"Verily I say unto you, Inasmuch as ye have done it unto one of the least of these my brethren, ye have done it unto me."* **[Matthew 25:40]**

♪ Let it be, let it be... ♪
All you need is love...
The Beatles

Conclusion Parts I & II

"God is with you, my brother. Let us join in Him in peace and gratitude, and accept His gift as our most holy and perfect reality, which we share in Him."
-A Course in Miracles [Text: chapter 18, section I, paragraph 10, sentence 8, 9]

"And the angel came in unto her, and said, Hail, thou that art highly favoured, the Lord is with thee: blessed art thou among women."
-Bible New Testament [Luke: chapter 1, verse 28]

"And the angel of the LORD appeared unto him, and said unto him, The LORD is with thee, thou mighty man of valour."
-Bible Old Testament [Judges: chapter 6, verse 12]

Given the fact that there is no such thing as different parts of my life because there is only one dream that appears to be fragmented in different parts, after practicing the principles outlined in this book, although I could say that I have noticed that my priorities have shifted, writing this book and sharing these teachings with others brings more joy than the comedy career, or music career I pursued so tenaciously in the past. That does not mean I may not produce music, write songs, put a band together or do anything in the artistic field in the future. However, *peace of mind is my most important priority.*

As I shared in a previous chapter, *I am better off losing everything I have and having my peace of mind than to have everything at the expense of losing my peace of mind.* So what exactly is it that you are doing when letting go? *You are now allowing the Holy Spirit to take over the projector.* That's how the Holy Spirit can replace your current nightmares (error in perception) with *happy dreams* (Holy Spirit's vision) through a change in perception.

How long will it take for you to experience these happy dreams (change in perception)? It all depends on how long you want to hang on to your attachments, ideas, values, concepts and beliefs. Because every time you hold on to something, it is like taking the projector from the Holy Spirit and giving it back to the ego. That's what we do throughout our lives. And the Holy Spirit will never force Itself upon anyone. All we need to do is to invite Him in by dropping our resistance. Until then, rest assured however, that sooner or later, the pain will be so unbearable that we will gladly handover the projector to the Holy Spirit. As *A Course in Miracles* reminds me, "*Tolerance for pain may be high, but it is not without limit. Eventually everyone begins to recognize, however dimly, that there must be a better way.*" **T-2.III.3:5-6**

Remember once again that the happy dream is *not* to be confused with better *illusions*. It is something that takes place at the level of the mind, *not* the form. If you think that a happy dream is having your material goals manifested, that is the same as to exchange one illusion for another, or one symbol for another and that is not liberation as *A Course in Miracles* reminds me, "*To change illusions is to make no change.*" **T-22.II.2:4**

The goal of The Course is to lead us out of this world of illusion while experiencing a peaceful and happy attitude. It just so happens that when we achieve a state of peacefulness, joy and happiness, the images that are taking place in our field of awareness are most likely to change, only that it wont make a difference in our attitude because we are already experiencing joy and happiness anyway.

> *All you need to give up is your psychological attachment to them. If you feel you have to give up something, then that is the same as sacrificing. But if you become detached, then it becomes a preference.*

A Course in Miracles reminds me: "*The happy dreams the Holy Spirit brings are different from the dreaming of the world, where one can merely dream he is awake. The dreams forgiveness lets the mind perceive **do not induce another form of sleep,** so that the dreamer dreams another dream. His happy dreams are heralds of the dawn of truth upon the mind. They lead from sleep to gentle waking, so that dreams are gone. And thus they cure for all eternity."* **W-pI.140.3:1-5**

So do you have to give up the things of this world? No, you don't have to give up anything. All you need to give up is your *psychological attachment* to them. If you feel you have to give up something, then that is the same as sacrificing. But if you become detached, then it becomes a *preference*. And just so you know, the process of forgiveness allows you to detach *gradually* from the things of this world so don't think this is a behavioral change or something you can do on your own. The Holy Spirit will help you along the way until the time comes when your values *naturally* shift towards God. So relax, just do your forgiveness process and trust.

In my case, I would prefer to have this book published, be able to speak worldwide, and have an abundant life doing just what I love. However, I am just not attached to any of my preferences, because I know these preferences are not my source of happiness and joy. And just because these are preferences, it does not mean that after the manuscript is finished, that I won't look for a publisher, or self-publish it, and that I won't make phone calls and promote it or network to get booked into places. The thing is, I *won't force* any of those things to happen. I'll simply do what I am *inspired* to do in each and every moment. While the manuscript is being published, what will I do in between to generate income? I don't know. I'll simply let go. And yes,

I have been putting out applications for work. I just haven't been called.

I would like to share something in regard to preferences that although is dualistic in nature I'll say it anyway so you can enjoy it. There is something about boats and the ocean that I just love. Last year, every time I drove by a particular boat dealer I had this urge to go in and get inside one of those boats, and feel what it would be like if I owned one. I also had this wonderful feeling of what it would be like to live in a boat at a marina. These are not goals; these are just thoughts that when I think of them bring me joy. I am not emotionally attached to them and my life is not less than perfect because they are not part of my experience. A few months ago, I was driving with Dawn and after we passed a boat dealership, I asked her if it would be okay to go in and look. She picked one that we both loved. I was asking all sorts of questions, I sat inside, and meditated on it. It was a wonderful experience and when we left the boat dealership, I just allowed myself to enjoy the experience and then let it go.

Last Wednesday was my last day at the place where I was allowed to stay while writing this book. As you can tell this chapter was written over a two-week period. And even today I am writing things that will be included in chapters that were written almost six months ago. But to continue with the story, after going to church that night, I saw my friend Aaron. In the conversation, I was just sharing what was taking place and asked him if he knew of a place where I could stay, and to keep his eyes open. He said to me with a grin on his face, *"my brother, I know exactly what you are going through because I have been there, so if you need a place to stay, you can stay with me."* Did I mention that he lives on a 40-foot sailboat docked in Marina Del Rey, California? What if I say to you that I am typing these words from his boat? In other words, I am living the *full* experience of being on a boat at the marina *without* costing me anything. It is like being given a preview of what it would be like should I decide to invest in a boat and live on it. Of course, I know that it is all an illusion and nothing means anything; the point is, look at the possible surprises when you let go.

I am certainly not saying that if you were in my situation you would have to do what I am doing. Just do whatever *feels appropriate to you*. As we continue undoing the ego, the time comes when no matter how much work we put into changing a particular circumstance or set of circumstances, the effort we put in seems to be wasted, as if all the doors we are trying to open are being blocked from us. The reason being is that if you remember from the six stages of developing trust, once we start the process of undoing the ego through forgiveness, and are *truly* willing to allow the Holy Spirit to guide us, these seeming setbacks are obstacles that are being brought to the surface to be healed, they are nothing more than distraction from the ego's thought system to keep our attention on our illusions instead of our peace.

The key to remember is to *do what we feel inspired to do*, to continue *practicing* forgiveness, so that we can experience *detachment*. The good news is there are no mistakes or wrong decisions. We don't have that power. In choosing the ego we are simply delaying our peace of mind. However, God will never allow us to get lost, even when sometimes we think we are.

Another thing I have discovered is that from my non-attachment, and by *not resisting anything*, aside from experiencing peace by not adding unnecessary stress and worry, I also tend to enjoy even more whatever experience I am having within the dream. Things I struggle for on the other hand, their illusory high washes away rather quickly because the reason I struggled for them was because I thought they had something of value to offer. Remember, I am still part of this illusion and there are experiences I would like to have; this time however, I am in a much different space.

Oh, by the way, remember a few paragraphs ago when I mentioned that once the book is published I will see what I will do in regard to finding work? And do you also remember when I said that since this book is being written over a period of months, some chapters were being updated as I went along? Right this moment the whole book is finished. I am just doing last proofreads and updates. As I am doing so, I also have a full time job at a printing factory which is not only about five minutes away from where I am living but it also came to me very easily when it was time for me to get a job. I have a few speaking engagements coming up, I'm in the process of contacting radio stations for interviews while sending a few preliminary copies of this book to authors. I am even considering the possibility of looking for a publisher. I am doing all that *without* being attached to specific results. As you can see, I am moving in the direction I am feeling inspired to, *always* remembering to let go because I *trust* that the Holy Spirit knows best.

I also want to mention that at the beginning of this book I shared that one of the reasons I was attracted to The Course was because it led me to answers *without* giving me *specific* answers. Also The Course helped me understand through Jesus' teachings that God did not create this world, *I did*, meaning the ego did. That's why I could never understand how a God that is all loving, compassionate, and giving could create a world filled with anger, hatred, and vengeance. In other words, how could a God of Oneness create a world that is filled with separation?

I share that with you because as I studied other philosophies and new age teachers, many of them, even when using words such as illusions to describe this world, still look at it as if this is the world that God created and they treat it as real. As I studied The Course and saw what was really taking place, who in his/her right mind would want to live in a world that is made up by an ego? It does not matter how pretty the illusion may look at times, why would someone want to experience all the suffering and the tragedy that comes along with this illusion? The answer is, someone who forgot Who he/she really is.

Judith Skutch Whitson, President and Chairperson of the Foundation for Inner Peace in an interview once said:

> "The course is predicated on two belief systems. One is real, the other is false. The false belief system is one the ego adheres to. And that is that we are born into this world, in physical bodies, in a world that is real, the physical, and things happens to us. And sometimes we experience happiness, once in a while joy, very often depression and anxiety, certainly disease, and always death. And that's the system of thought that the ego loves, the ego adheres to, the ego exalts, and the ego wants us to believe in.
> On the other hand, there is the belief system that God is our reality. We are created in God's image as Spirits, not the physical body. That we are love. That a property of love is light, and that we are eternal. We can't be hurt or inviolate. We

can't be destroyed. When one puts it that way, **who but an insane person would want to choose the ego."**

To find out more about Judith Skutch Whitson's work, visit: *www.acim.org*. After my strict religious upbringing, another thing I love about A Course in Miracles is the fact that it says that *you don't need* The Course, that all you need to do is to simply come with wholly empty hands unto your God as The Course reminds me when it says, *"Forget this world, **forget this course**, and come with wholly empty hands unto your God."* **W-pI.189.7:5**

> *"Forget this world, forget this course, and come with wholly empty hands unto your God.*

Honestly speaking, if you get what that lesson is asking us to do, and *truly live it*, you *don't need anything else.* You can take this book, put it back on your shelf or just give it away, for this book, or any other book, teacher or seminar would have *nothing* else to offer. However, since the ego is so complicated, here is something I have decided to share now that may be hard for most teachers to accept. But after what you have read, assuming you have read this whole book, and maybe after being shocked many times over, here is something else for you to digest.

We hear a lot about making unconscious decisions. That is why people work on changing whatever is taking place unconsciously thinking that decisions could be made at that level. What if I said to you that it is *impossible* to make an unconscious decision? And that every decision we make is actually a *conscious* one? Why would I say so? Let's begin by reading some excerpts from The Course.

> **"Defenses are not unintentional,** *nor are they made without awareness. They are secret, magic wands you wave when truth appears to threaten what you would believe."* **W-pI.136.3:1-2**

If we are in the midst of an illusion, the body is an illusion, our brain is an illusion, is there such a thing as an unconscious mind? The answer would be, no. One Mind is all that there is, and it is the Mind of God. What we have however are *beliefs*, and when those beliefs are threatened by truth, we automatically *react* and become defensive. Then it goes on to say;

> *"They seem to be unconscious but because of the **rapidity with which you choose to use them**. In that second, even less, in which the choice is made, **you recognize exactly** what you would attempt to do, and proceed to think that it is done."* **W-pI.136.3:4-4**

So what seems like an unconscious choice is really a *conscious* one, but because of the fact that it was made so *fast*, it seemed as if it was made without your conscious awareness. In the next paragraph, The Course says;

> *"Who but yourself evaluates a threat, decides escape is necessary, and sets up a series of defenses to reduce the threat that has been judged as real? **All this cannot be done unconsciously**. But afterwards, **your plan requires that you must forget you made it**, so it seems to be external to your own intent; a happening beyond your state of mind, an outcome with a real effect on you, instead of one effected by yourself."* **W-pI.136.4:1-3**

In other words, the fact that you made a very fast decision by reacting to a situation that you thought was real was a *conscious* decision. However in order for you to *convince* yourself that the decision was made unconsciously, the ego's plan requires that you *forget* the fact that *you are the one* who made the decision. So every decision we make, whether we choose to believe it or not, is a decision made consciously. The difference is, to the degree that we are becoming more and more aware, by handing over our thoughts to the Holy Spirit first, the time gap between an illusion that we project and the way we respond to it lengthens. Therefore, through the practice of forgiveness, we give ourselves the opportunity to let the Holy Spirit undo the guilt that gave rise to the interpretation that made us react without having to dissect or change anything in the subconscious mind, which *does not* exist in the first place. Only one thing exists, and that is God. Everything else is an illusion. That's why it is said, *God Is.*

If you are new to these teachings or even someone who has been on the spiritual path for a long time, I am not going to deny that this book may have challenged a lot of the beliefs you've cherished dearly. I know the feeling. However, for me, all I am interested in is Truth, *not* beliefs. I had to let go of all I thought I knew. You may or may not be ready to make this decision fully and that is okay too. *A Course in Miracles* reminds me: *"Heaven is **chosen** consciously. The choice **cannot** be made **until** alternatives are accurately seen and understood."* **W-pI.138.9:1-2** In other words, choosing the path to awakening cannot be made until we are willing and ready to choose nothing else but God. The alternatives are the false idols we look up to. The illusions we are still attached to. For me, after attending seminar after seminar, studying with teacher after teacher, reading book after book, listening to tape after tape, watching movie after movie, and still not experiencing true peace, that's when I became ready to make the *conscious* decision to choose Heaven, in other words, to let go.

> *"Heaven is chosen consciously. The choice cannot be made until alternatives are accurately seen and understood."*

If I were to sum up this whole book, I can think of four things:

1. The world is an illusion, just an outward representation of an inward condition. It is our *belief* that we are separate from one another, which is symbolic of our separation from God, when in reality we are all One.

2. In order to release ourselves from that idea of separation, all we need to do is to practice forgiveness, while remembering that the *only* one we are forgiving is ourselves. Not for having done something wrong, but for the fact that we have not done anything, therefore we are innocent. As a result of our forgiveness, our sense of guilt is forever removed from our unconscious. In that sense all of our projections disappear.

3. To make peace our *most* important priority. Suggestions on how to do so would be by:
    - resisting *nothing*.
    - *practicing* forgiveness.
    - *not* attempting to give meaning to *anything*.
    - accepting people, situations and circumstances *just as they are*.
    - offering *all* our fears and concerns to the Holy Spirit for reinterpretation.
    - *trusting* the fact that *everything* is unfolding as it should be, and if in doubt remember Gary Renard's words; *"...when things don't look the way I expect them to, it's time to **stop questioning** and **start trusting.**"*

4. As a result of that inner transformation we stop taking this *world* seriously, because *none of it is real!*

That being said, this book is *not* a replacement for *A Course in Miracles*. To me, it is simply an opportunity to share what *my* experience has been as a result of putting the principles of The Course into practice, and how it has affected my life. As I mentioned towards the beginning of this book, I was introduced to The Course many years ago. However, if it had not been first for Gary Renard's book *The Disappearance of the Universe*, followed by Dr. Kenneth Wapnick's impeccable understanding and explanation of the Course's teachings through the *Foundation for A Course in Miracles* at www.facim.org, I would not have been able to understand its teachings. Especially since many teachers have quoted from The Course to fit their individual curriculums. That's why The Course reminds me: *"I have made every effort to use words that are **almost impossible to distort,** but it is always possible **to twist symbols around if you wish.**"* T-3.I.3:11 In a conversation between Dr. Jeffrey Moses and Mother Teresa she said to him, *"God has a special purpose for every action. People's individual desires and egos, however, often distort this."*

This book was written because as I was touched by the content of *A Course in Miracles*, and having the *direct* experience of what The Course teaches in many areas in my life, the teacher in me could not help himself, but to share the gift that The Course has given me. That

being said, remember that this book is *also* a *symbol*, and if you look up to me, or within the words contained in this book for answers, then you may end up losing yourself because *only* the Holy Spirit has the one answer that would solve your only "seeming" problem. As *A Course in Miracles* reminds me, "*It is not difficult to understand the reasons why you do not ask the Holy Spirit to solve all problems for you. He has not greater difficulty in resolving some than others. Every problem is the same to Him, because each one is solved in just the same respect and through the same approach. The aspects that need solving do not change, whatever form the problem seems to take. A problem can appear in many forms, and it will do so while the problem lasts. It serves no purpose to attempt to solve it in a special form. It will recur and then recur again and yet again, until it has been answered for all time and will not rise again in any form. And only then are you released from it.*" **T-26.II.1:1-8**
. I just serve as a *reminder* so when you are tempted to look for answers out in the world (illusion), to just *turn within* and know *therein lies God*.

If you resonated with what I have shared in this book, and feel inspired to read The Course, let the Voice Within decide for you, *always* remembering that The Course is just *one* path out of *many*. As I quoted from The Course before, and it is worth repeating, *A Course in Miracles* reminds me: *"...The Course deals with universal spiritual themes. It emphasizes that it is but **one version** of the universal curriculum. **There are many others**, this one differing from them only in form. They all lead to God in the end."* ACIM Preface Just to demonstrate how deceiving the ego is, I am going to share one last time, few excerpts from Jeffrey Moses' book titled *Oneness, Great Principles Shared By All Religions*:

Islam: *"There are as many ways to God as souls; as many as the breaths of Adam's sons.'*
Hinduism: *"They who worship other gods with faith,*
              They adore but me behind those forms;
              Many are the paths of men,
              But they all in the end come to me."
Christianity: *"For as many as are led by the Spirit of God, they are sons of God."*

Confucianism: *"Confucius said: 'In the world there are many different roads, but the destination is the same.'"*

Pawnee, Native American: *"All religions are but stepping-stones back to God."*

Notice how many people try to convert others to their own faith, as if their path is the only one, even when *their own* scriptures suggest that there are many paths to God.

People often employ the teachings of the Bible amongst other books, in an attempt to not only understand what Jesus was all about, but to also try to be like Him. Having Jesus the Christ as my teacher, with nothing less than *unconditional love* for you, I choose to end this book sharing these words from the Master Himself as stated in *A Course in Miracles*;

> *"There is nothing about me that you cannot attain. I have nothing that does not come from God.* ***The difference between us now is, that I have nothing else.*** *This leaves me in a state which is only potential to you."* –**J. Christ** T-1.II.3:10-13

I want to remind you, once again, that *you are exactly where you need to be* and that *everything is truly working together for your highest good*. All you need to do is to continue developing *trust*, which reminds me of something I wrote back in 1995:

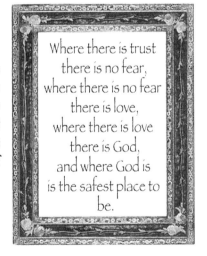

Where there is trust there is no fear, where there is no fear there is love, where there is love there is God, and where God is is the safest place to be.

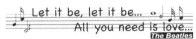

> "There is nothing about me that you cannot attain. I have nothing that does not come from God. **The difference between us now is, that I have nothing else**. This leaves me in a state which is only potential to you." –J. Christ T-1.II.3:10-13

...and the journey continues...

About the Author

There was a time when I thought I needed to have an extensive resume filled with a long list of credentials and accomplishments in order to impress others. Then I came to the realization that if there is One I would want to impress, that would be God. So, although I seem to have a lot of things that would conjure up an impressive resume, I'll let you watch my biography on video at my website: *www.TruthAndMiracles.com*.

As far as where I am in my life, all I can say is that *I Am*. Every morning when I wake up, I remind myself that I know nothing. Then when I go to bed at night, once again I remind myself that I know nothing. And during the day I simply ask God:

"*What would You have me do?*
Where would You have me go?
What would You have me say, and to whom?" **W-pI.71.9:3-5**

A Course in Miracles reminds me: "*...let Him tell you what needs to be done by you in His plan for your salvation.*" **W-pI.71.9:6** The scriptures also remind me: "*It is better to trust in the Lord than to put confidence in man,*" **[Psalms 118:8]** And if you would like to know *Who you really are*, here is a story told by a dear Reverend at one of his Sunday services.

A man found himself in the gates of Heaven after making his transition. He knocked on the door and God asked; "*Who is it?*" The man replied; "*It's me, Peter.*" God said, "*Go away, there is no room for you here.*" Peter knocked again and once more God asked; "*Who is it?*" And Peter once again replied, "*It's me Peter. Don't you remember me? The one who has done so many great things in the world, healed lots of people, loved everyone and forgave everyone?*" And God once again said, "*Go away, there is no room for you here.*" Peter very disappointed and confused went away and in tears started to pray. Then he received an insight. So he went back and knocked on the door. God once again asked; "*Who is it?*" And Peter said; "*I am Thou.*" God opened the gate and said, "*Come on in Peter. There is no room for me and you, there is only room for me **as** you.*"

Additional Support

If you enjoyed this book and would like to put into practice the principles of true surrender and trust, Nick has written a companion to *What Happens When You Let God* entitled ***I Am Workbook***.

For information on how to order as well as to read book's excerpts visit:

www.IAmWorkbook.com

Suggested Readings

A Course in Miracles is available in hardcover, tradepaper, and paperback English editions as well, translated in fourteen different languages. The latest edition consists of the original Text, Workbook for Students, Manual for Teachers along with two addendums, which are *The Song of Prayer* as an extension of the principles of The Course and *Psychotherapy: Purpose, Process and Practice*. For more information write or call: *Foundation for Inner Peace P.O. Box 598, Mill Valley, CA 94942-0598 (415) 388-2620* To find out more about The Course visit their website at: ***www.acim.org***

Although throughout this book I have quoted briefly from other authors because I felt that what they were saying was congruent with the topic in discussion, I don't want to send any mix signals, especially to students who've been drawn to the teachings of *A Course in Miracles*. As you practice trusting your inner guidance, you will be led to a book, teacher, or resource that is perfect for you. As for me, the following books are written by authors, that aside from being *A Course in Miracles'* students/teachers, through their work, they have made a *positive impact* in my life.

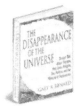

The Disappearance of the Universe by **Gary Renard** is a *must* read for every modern day disciple of *A Course in Miracles*. To find out more about Gary's work visit his website at: ***www.GaryRenard.com***. "This book is the one that helped me understand the teachings of *A Course in Miracles*." –Nick Arandes

Any books, videos or audios by **Kenneth Wapnick**, *which is considered to be the most influential and knowledgeable teacher of A Course in Miracles. You can find out all about him by visiting:* ***www.facim.org***.

Additional Resources

A Foundation of *A Course in Miracles* by Gloria and Kenneth Wapnick. The principal purpose of the foundation is to help students of *A Course in Miracles* deepen their understanding of its thought system, conceptually and experientially, so that they may be more effective instruments of Jesus' teaching in their own particular lives. For information on the foundation visit their website at: ***www.facim.org***.

"I feel that Dr. Ken Wapnick is one of the most qualified, knowledgeable and dedicated teachers of A Course in Miracles in the world today." –Nick Arandes, May 2009

ACIM Mentor by **Liz Cronkhite** is a resource for serious students of *A Course in Miracles* who want to more quickly and easily integrate The Course's principles in their life or if they simply wish to gain a clearer, deeper understanding of The Course. To learn more about her experience simply visit: ***www.ACIMMentor.com***.

"If you have a chance, subscribe to her newsletter, which is filled with simple, yet very profound wisdom from her experience as a student and teacher of A Course in Miracles." –Nick Arandes

Book Nick To Speak

Nick Arandes is by far one of the most dynamic speakers in the circuit today. He is affectionately known as the *Radical Kid* for a reason. His off the wall, great sense of humor, and unique way to present *powerful* spiritual principles, helps accelerate people's personal transformation. His presentations are not only based on true spiritual principles but most importantly, *personal experience.*

> "Nick, it's wonderful to hear from you. We always love it when you are here, you are truly gifted. One thing I can share with you now is a note that was in the collection;
> 'DAVID - THE SPEAKER YOU HAD TODAY WAS GREAT. YOU HAVE A GREAT THING GOING. SHOWS YOUR CONSCIOUSNESS - GREAT.' -Rev. Dr. Warren C.
> That's right, we only have the best here at our church! Thank you for holding a high vision for me, one I intend to live up to! Many Blessings to you," -Theresa L.

> "Nick, Your presence and your talk today at the Pasadena Church of Religious Science was truly a gift, a blessing, tons of fun, inspiring and enlightening! If God's the answer, what's the question? You are the manifestation of many miracles! Love and Light," Rev. Jeanne S.

To find out more about having Nick speak or facilitate a workshop at your event, place of worship or any special engagement simply visit his site at:

www.TruthAndMiracles.com
www.NickArandes.com

If you are interested in finding out about Nick's music just visit his music site at:

www.CheckMyMusic.com

Testimonials

"...Nazirah, our member informs me that almost 500 people attended the event and the feedback has been extremely positive. In particular, the people were amazed at your multi talents, especially your ability to invoke so much laughter and simultaneously inspire them to follow their heart's desires!" –M. Z. Council for British Columbia

"Hi Nick, thank you for being a part of the first ever event this past Sunday in Vancouver. I was part of the team and had every intention of thanking you personally for sharing 'you' with us; however, I did not get a chance to do so and am therefore sending you an email. So, Nick, thank you for an awe inspiring hour of sharing with us your life and your wisdom. I laughed and I cried....and I felt you touch a part of me. Thank you" -Annar

"BRAVO! BRAVO! BRAVO! You are an excellent speaker and you offer so much for thought and action. You are a terrific person, and I was, /am totally inspired by your larger-than-life persona. All blessings, always! " -Marianne A., IN

"I would love to attend future programs of yours. I have also been talking to my friends about you. I was very much impressed. With best wishes for success in your life, I am sure you have touched many hearts. Please continue to do what you are doing at the moment. God bless you," -Gulshan

"Hi Nick, "GREAT WORDS, GREAT THINKER, AND AS A RESULT GREAT DOER" -Janasan

"I am glad to know about your dreams throughout your values, mission and vision; however, your presence in seminars inspired me... Please, keep in your mind, heart, soul, and spirit, you have a good friend in me... In tone with the Universe, we share blessings..." -Javier N.

"The organization and the calibre of speakers surmounted the expectations of those that attended. I was encouraged to pass on feedback to encourage our leadership to host more events such as the one today. I believe there were many new relationships built and old ones rekindled. Many left with thoughts and ideas to reflect on. People were extremely impressed with Nick Arandes." - Shairose

Nick, every time I read or listen to something of yours, that's what I feel all over again - at-one-ment. Thank you! Cheryl Y.

Dear Nick, I live in South Africa and "accidently" came across your website recently. Of course there are no accidents and I understand that I manifested you in my life as a result of the spiritual journey I am on. I am inspired on a daily basis and am very grateful for that. I wish you all future success and favor on your journey as well as the effect you have on other people's journeys. Namaste -John. A.

I've been listening to your inspirational messages probably since you've been doing them and each time I listen I can't belive how the messages relate to my life. It's really amazing. -Alena M.

Hi Nick! I just wanted to say that the stuff you teach is the best in the world!!! I rarely say this about anyone. I think you are teaching from the highest level of all things. The level of spirit. You are the master's master. Best Regards, Enoch T.

Hi Nick, (you rock!) First of all, I would like to express my appreciation for your wonderful insights and excellent website that has helped me move from living what was a negative environment into an appreciative wonderful life. Keep on being the way you are, reaching so many people and not changing the way you deliver your message! It is helping me!!!!! Love, Penny

Dear Nick: I am writing from Guatemala. I want to tell you how wonderful it is to learn from you. You keep reminding me of who I am. It is wonderful to have persons (I should say spirits) like you helping us to remember our real being. Thank you very much, keep doing what you came to do here. We hear from you every day. If you want to come to Guatemala, be sure you have a place to stay. We all love you, keep in track. Martha A.

Dear Nick. I'm so glad to know you little bit better! I love your style, what you teach and how, resonates with me. I discovered you not too long ago! I'm recommending you to my friends. Good Luck, God Bless, your newest student.... Jolanta

Hi dear Nick, you are so passionate, intriguing, straight-forward and provoking, truly extraordinary - I really appreciate and love that. Annette, Germany

Hi Nick, I listen to/watch many spiritual & motivational speakers and enjoy them all. However, you are the first person I've come across who's message resonates totally with my own experiences. I'm happy you're on the planet and pleased I've discovered you and your message. Kind regards, Linda S., New Zealand

Good Morning Nick, I am very much enjoying "my creation" of you, as God / The Universe is always speaking to me through you. Your words are music to my soul. Much love and happiness to you today -- and have a great one! Jodi, CA

Wow, Nick... Thank you so much for your kindness and up-lifting message. You have a rare and special gift! -Michelle

Nick, Since I met you, God has blessed me in so many ways and I thank you and appreciate you more than you can imagine. This is an amazing journey and so special to me. Thanks again for giving me this opportunity. Take care. Many Blessings to You. D. J., Hawaii

I can't even begin to describe how it affects me when I listen to you. Beyond inspirational. Thank you Nick. Sincerely, -Diane D.

Dear Nick, Out of all the people featured on the Life and Love TV site [spirituality] you were the last person who's video I watched. I had gone there to watch (name undisclosed) and listen to what he had to say. I still felt thirsty for more inspirational talks afterwards, so I watched all the other videos. Well, perhaps God did save the best til last! :-) I've just listened to you and wanted to say 'thank you'. I appreciate your message, your perspective, your wisdom and your enthusiasm and grateful I've discovered you. Linda

Dear Nick, I really, really, really enjoyed your talk. I get your emails and I went to listen because I think you have great things to say. You nailed my belief system and I know I was meant to hear it today. My life has been getting better and better and better and today I woke up with a sense of wanting to connect all day with my divine intelligence. Bless you and thank you again. -Luchy G., CA

Nick, Thanks for following your heart and intuition. We are entering an era to bring people back to themselves. Continue to let the light shine through you. Thanks for reminding me to trust the Universe ALWAYS has better plans for my future. -Ann W.

"Your insight I know comes from the Power and the Presence of God." - Mike P., CT

MANY MORE TESTIMONIALS AVAILABLE UPON REQUEST

Made in the USA
Lexington, KY
06 August 2015